Fanny's First Play

George Bernard Shaw

Fanny's First Play

George Bernard Shaw

© 1st World Library – Literary Society, 2004
PO Box 2211
Fairfield, IA 52556
www.1stworldlibrary.org
First Edition

LCCN: 2003099913

ISBN: 1-59540-242-X

Purchase *"Fanny's First Play"*
as a traditional bound book at:
www.1stWorldLibrary.org/purchase.asp?ISBN=1-59540-242-X

1st World Library Literary Society is a nonprofit
organization dedicated to promoting literacy by:

- Creating a free internet library accessible from any
  computer worldwide.
- Hosting writing competitions and offering book
  publishing scholarships.

Readers interested in supporting literacy
through sponsorship, donations or
membership please contact:
literacy@1stworldlibrary.org
Check us out at: www.1stworldlibrary.org

Fanny's First Play
contributed by the Charles Family
in support of
1st World Library Literary Society

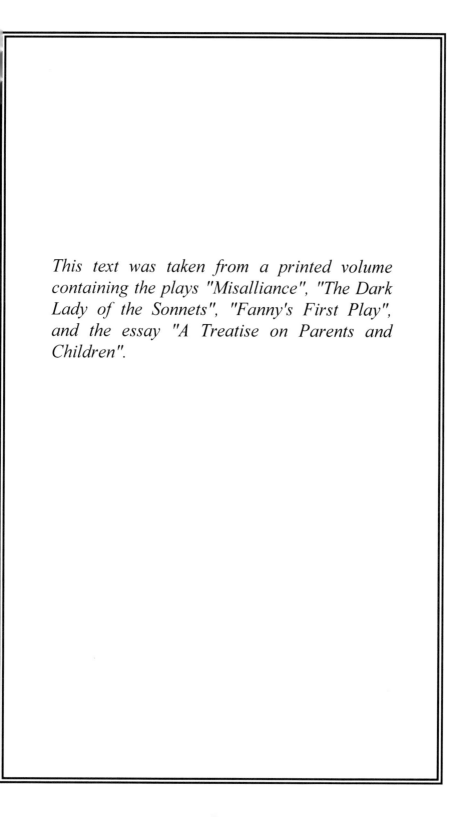

This text was taken from a printed volume containing the plays "Misalliance", "The Dark Lady of the Sonnets", "Fanny's First Play", and the essay "A Treatise on Parents and Children".

PREFACE TO FANNY'S FIRST PLAY

Fanny's First Play, being but a potboiler, needs no preface. But its lesson is not, I am sorry to say, unneeded. Mere morality, or the substitution of custom for conscience was once accounted a shameful and cynical thing: people talked of right and wrong, of honor and dishonor, of sin and grace, of salvation and damnation, not of morality and immorality. The word morality, if we met it in the Bible, would surprise us as much as the word telephone or motor car. Nowadays we do not seem to know that there is any other test of conduct except morality; and the result is that the young had better have their souls awakened by disgrace, capture by the police, and a month's hard labor, than drift along from their cradles to their graves doing what other people do for no other reason than that other people do it, and knowing nothing of good and evil, of courage and cowardice, or indeed anything but how to keep hunger and concupiscence and fashionable dressing within the bounds of good taste except when their excesses can be concealed. Is it any wonder that I am driven to offer to young people in our suburbs the desperate advice: Do something that will get you into trouble? But please do not suppose that I defend a state of things which makes such advice the best that can be given under the circumstances, or that I do not know how difficult it is to find out a way of getting into trouble that will combine loss of respectability with integrity of self-respect and reasonable consideration for other peoples' feelings and interests on every point except their dread of losing their own respectability. But when there's a will there's a way. I hate to see dead people walking about: it is unnatural. And our respectable middle class people are all as dead as mutton. Out of the mouth of Mrs Knox I have delivered on them the judgment of her God.

The critics whom I have lampooned in the induction to this play under the names of Trotter, Vaughan, and Gunn will forgive me: in fact Mr Trotter forgave me beforehand, and assisted the make-up by which Mr Claude King so successfully simulated his personal appearance. The critics whom I did not introduce were somewhat hurt, as I should have been myself under the same circumstances; but I had not room for them all; so I can only apologize and assure them that I meant no disrespect.

The concealment of the authorship, if a secret de Polichinelle can be said to involve concealment, was a necessary part of the play. In so far as it was effectual, it operated as a measure of relief to those critics and playgoers who are so obsessed by my strained legendary reputation that they approach my plays in a condition which is really one of derangement, and are quite unable to conceive a play of mine as anything but a trap baited with paradoxes, and designed to compass their ethical perversion and intellectual confusion. If it were possible, I should put forward all my plays anonymously, or hire some less disturbing person, as Bacon is said to have hired Shakespear, to father my plays for me.

George Bernard Shaw

Fanny's First Play was performed for the first time at the Little Theatre in the Adelphi, London, on the afternoon of Wednesday, April 19th 1911.

INDUCTION

The end of a saloon in an old-fashioned country house (Florence Towers, the property of Count O'Dowda) has been curtained off to form a stage for a private theatrical performance. A footman in grandiose Spanish livery enters before the curtain, on its O.P. side.

FOOTMAN. [announcing] Mr Cecil Savoyard. [Cecil Savoyard comes in: a middle-aged man in evening dress and a fur-lined overcoat. He is surprised to find nobody to receive him. So is the Footman]. Oh, beg pardon, sir: I thought the Count was here. He was when I took up your name. He must have gone through the stage into the library. This way, sir. [He moves towards the division in the middle of the curtains].

SAVOYARD. Half a mo. [The Footman stops]. When does the play begin? Half-past eight?

FOOTMAN. Nine, sir.

SAVOYARD. Oh, good. Well, will you telephone to my wife at the George that it's not until nine?

FOOTMAN. Right, sir. Mrs Cecil Savoyard, sir?

SAVOYARD. No: Mrs William Tinkler. Dont forget.

THE FOOTMAN. Mrs Tinkler, sir. Right, sir. [The Count comes in through the curtains]. Here is the Count, sir. [Announcing] Mr Cecil Savoyard, sir. [He withdraws].

COUNT O'DOWDA. [A handsome man of fifty, dressed with studied elegance a hundred years out of date, advancing cordially to shake hands with his visitor] Pray excuse me, Mr Savoyard. I suddenly recollected that all the bookcases in the library were locked - in fact theyve never been opened since we came from Venice - and as our literary guests will probably use the library a good deal, I just ran in to unlock everything.

SAVOYARD. Oh, you mean the dramatic critics. M'yes. I suppose theres a smoking room?

THE COUNT. My study is available. An old-fashioned house, you understand. Wont you sit down, Mr Savoyard?

SAVOYARD. Thanks. [They sit. Savoyard, looking at his host's obsolete costume, continues] I had no idea you were going to appear in the piece yourself.

THE COUNT. I am not. I wear this costume because - well, perhaps I had better explain the position, if it interests you.

SAVOYARD. Certainly.

THE COUNT. Well, you see, Mr Savoyard, I'm rather a stranger in your world. I am not, I hope, a modern man in any sense of the word. I'm not really an Englishman: my family is Irish: Ive lived all my life in

Italy - in Venice mostly - my very title is a foreign one: I am a Count of the Holy Roman Empire.

SAVOYARD. Where's that?

THE COUNT. At present, nowhere, except as a memory and an ideal. [Savoyard inclines his head respectfully to the ideal]. But I am by no means an idealogue. I am not content with beautiful dreams: I want beautiful realities.

SAVOYARD. Hear, hear! I'm all with you there - when you can get them.

THE COUNT. Why not get them? The difficulty is not that there are no beautiful realities, Mr Savoyard: the difficulty is that so few of us know them when we see them. We have inherited from the past a vast treasure of beauty - of imperishable masterpieces of poetry, of painting, of sculpture, of architecture, of music, of exquisite fashions in dress, in furniture, in domestic decoration. We can contemplate these treasures. We can reproduce many of them. We can buy a few inimitable originals. We can shut out the nineteenth century -

SAVOYARD. [correcting him] The twentieth.

THE COUNT. To me the century I shut out will always be the nineteenth century, just as your national anthem will always be God Save the Queen, no matter how many kings may succeed. I found England befouled with industrialism: well, I did what Byron did: I simply refused to live in it. You remember Byron's words: "I am sure my bones would not rest in an English grave, or my clay mix with the earth of that country. I believe the thought would drive me mad on my deathbed could I suppose that any of my friends would be base enough to convey my carcase back to her soil. I would not even feed her worms if I could help it."

SAVOYARD. Did Byron say that?

THE COUNT. He did, sir.

SAVOYARD. It dont sound like him. I saw a good deal of him at one time.

THE COUNT. You! But how is that possible? You are too young.

SAVOYARD. I was quite a lad, of course. But I had a job in the original production of Our Boys.

THE COUNT. My dear sir, not that Byron. Lord Byron, the poet.

SAVOYARD. Oh, I beg your pardon. I thought you were talking of the Byron. So you prefer living abroad?

THE COUNT. I find England ugly and Philistine. Well, I dont live in it. I find modern houses ugly. I dont live in them: I have a palace on the grand canal. I find modern clothes prosaic. I dont wear them, except, of course, in the street. My ears are offended by the Cockney twang: I keep out of hearing of it and speak and listen to Italian. I find Beethoven's music coarse and restless, and Wagner's senseless and detestable. I do not listen to them. I listen to Cimarosa, to Pergolesi, to Gluck and Mozart. Nothing simpler, sir.

SAVOYARD. It's all right when you can afford it.

THE COUNT. Afford it! My dear Mr Savoyard, if you are a man with a sense of beauty you can make an earthly paradise for yourself in Venice on 1500 pounds a year, whilst our wretched vulgar industrial millionaires are spending twenty thousand on the amusements of billiard markers. I assure you I am a poor man according to modern ideas. But I have never had anything less than the very best that life has produced. It is my good fortune to have a beautiful and lovable daughter; and that girl, sir, has never seen an ugly sight or heard an ugly sound that I could spare her; and she has certainly never worn an ugly dress or tasted coarse food or bad wine in her life. She has lived in a palace; and her perambulator was a gondola. Now you know the sort of people we are, Mr Savoyard. You can imagine how we feel here.

SAVOYARD. Rather out of it, eh?

THE COUNT. Out of it, sir! Out of what?

SAVOYARD. Well, out of everything.

THE COUNT. Out of soot and fog and mud and east wind; out of vulgarity and ugliness, hypocrisy and greed, superstition and stupidity. Out of all this, and in the sunshine, in the enchanted region of which great artists alone have had the secret, in the sacred footsteps of Byron, of Shelley, of the Brownings, of Turner and Ruskin. Dont you envy me, Mr Savoyard?

SAVOYARD. Some of us must live in England, you know, just to keep the place going. Besides - though, mind you, I dont say it isnt all right from the high art point of view and all that - three weeks of it would drive me melancholy mad. However, I'm glad you told me, because it explains why it is you dont seem to know your way about much in England. I hope, by the way, that everything has given satisfaction to your daughter.

THE COUNT. She seems quite satisfied. She tells me that the actors you sent down are perfectly suited to their parts, and very nice people to work with. I understand she had some difficulties at the first rehearsals with the gentleman you call the producer, because he hadnt read the play; but the moment he found out what it was all about everything went smoothly.

SAVOYARD. Havnt you seen the rehearsals?

THE COUNT. Oh no. I havnt been allowed even to meet any of the company. All I can tell you is that the hero is a Frenchman [Savoyard is rather scandalized]: I asked her not to have an English hero. That is all I know. [Ruefully] I havnt been consulted even about the costumes, though there, I think, I could have been some use.

SAVOYARD. [puzzled] But there arnt any costumes.

THE COUNT. [seriously shocked] What! No costumes! Do you mean to say it is a modern play?

SAVOYARD. I dont know: I didnt read it. I handed it to Billy Burjoyce - the producer, you know - and left it to him to select the company and so on. But I should have had to order the costumes if there had been any. There wernt.

THE COUNT. [smiling as he recovers from his alarm] I understand. She has taken the costumes into her own hands. She is an expert in beautiful costumes. I venture to promise you, Mr Savoyard, that what you are about to see will be like a Louis Quatorze ballet painted by Watteau. The heroine will be an exquisite Columbine, her lover a dainty Harlequin, her father a picturesque Pantaloon, and the valet who hoodwinks the father and brings about the happiness of the lovers a grotesque but perfectly tasteful Punchinello or Mascarille or Sganarelle.

SAVOYARD. I see. That makes three men; and the clown and policeman will make five. Thats why you wanted five men in the company.

THE COUNT. My dear sir, you dont suppose I mean that vulgar, ugly, silly, senseless, malicious and destructive thing, the harlequinade of a nineteenth century English Christmas pantomime! What was it after all but a stupid attempt to imitate the success made by the genius of Grimaldi a hundred years ago? My daughter does not know of the existence of such a thing. I refer to the graceful and charming fantasies of the Italian and French stages of the seventeenth and eighteenth centuries.

SAVOYARD. Oh, I beg pardon. I quite agree that harlequinades are rot. Theyve been dropped at all smart theatres. But from what Billy Burjoyce told me I got the idea that your daughter knew her way about here, and had seen a lot of plays. He had no idea she'd been away in Venice all the time.

THE COUNT. Oh, she has not been. I should have explained that two years ago my daughter left me to complete her education at Cambridge. Cambridge was my own University; and though of course there were no women there in my time, I felt confident that if the atmosphere of the eighteenth century still existed anywhere in England, it would be at Cambridge. About three months ago she wrote to me and asked whether I wished to give her a present on her next birthday. Of course I said yes; and she then astonished and delighted me by telling me that she had written a play, and that the present she wanted was a private performance of it with real actors and real critics.

SAVOYARD. Yes: thats what staggered me. It was easy enough to engage a company for a private performance: it's done often enough. But the notion of having critics was new. I hardly knew how to set about it. They dont expect private engagements; and so they have no agents. Besides, I didnt know what to offer them. I knew that they were cheaper than actors, because they get long engagements: forty years sometimes; but thats no rule for a single job. Then theres such a lot of them: on first nights they run away with all your stalls: you cant find a decent place for your own mother. It would have cost a fortune to bring the lot.

THE COUNT. Of course I never dreamt of having them all. Only a few first-rate representative men.

SAVOYARD. Just so. All you want is a few sample opinions. Out of a hundred notices you wont find more than four at the outside that say anything different. Well, Ive got just the right four for you. And what do you think it has cost me?

THE COUNT. [shrugging his shoulders] I cannot guess.

SAVOYARD. Ten guineas, and expenses. I had to give Flawner Bannal ten. He wouldnt come for less; and he asked fifty. I had to give it, because if we hadnt had him we might just as well have had nobody at all.

THE COUNT. But what about the others, if Mr Flannel -

SAVOYARD. [shocked] Flawner Bannal.

THE COUNT. - if Mr Bannal got the whole ten?

SAVOYARD. Oh, I managed that. As this is a high-class sort of thing, the first man I went for was Trotter.

THE COUNT. Oh indeed. I am very glad you have secured Mr Trotter. I have read his Playful Impressions.

SAVOYARD. Well, I was rather in a funk about him. Hes not exactly what I call approachable; and he was a bit stand-off at first. But when I explained and told him your daughter -

THE COUNT. [interrupting in alarm] You did not say that the play was by her, I hope?

SAVOYARD. No: thats been kept a dead secret. I just said your daughter has asked for a real play with a real author and a real critic and all the rest of it. The moment I mentioned the daughter I had him. He has a daughter of his own. Wouldnt hear of payment! Offered to come just to please her! Quite human. I was surprised.

THE COUNT. Extremely kind of him.

SAVOYARD. Then I went to Vaughan, because he does music as well as the drama: and you said you thought there would be music. I told him Trotter would feel lonely without him; so he promised like a bird. Then I thought youd like one of the latest sort: the chaps that go for the newest things and swear theyre oldfashioned. So I nailed Gilbert Gunn. The four will give you a representative team. By the way [looking at his watch] theyll be here presently.

THE COUNT. Before they come, Mr Savoyard, could you give me any hints about them that would help me to make a little conversation with them? I am, as you said, rather out of it in England; and I might unwittingly say something tactless.

SAVOYARD. Well, let me see. As you dont like English people, I don't know that youll get on with Trotter, because hes thoroughly English: never happy except when hes in Paris, and speaks French so unnecessarily well that everybody there spots him as an Englishman the moment he opens his mouth. Very witty and all that. Pretends to turn up his nose at the theatre and says people make too much fuss about art [the Count is extremely indignant]. But thats only his modesty, because art is his own line, you understand. Mind you dont chaff him about Aristotle.

THE COUNT. Why should I chaff him about Aristotle?

SAVOYARD. Well, I don't know; but its one of the

recognized ways of chaffing him. However, youll get on with him all right: hes a man of the world and a man of sense. The one youll have to be careful about is Vaughan.

THE COUNT. In what way, may I ask?

SAVOYARD. Well, Vaughan has no sense of humor; and if you joke with him he'll think youre insulting him on purpose. Mind: it's not that he doesnt see a joke: he does; and it hurts him. A comedy scene makes him sore all over: he goes away black and blue, and pitches into the play for all hes worth.

THE COUNT. But surely that is a very serious defect in a man of his profession?

SAVOYARD. Yes it is, and no mistake. But Vaughan is honest, and don't care a brass farthing what he says, or whether it pleases anybody or not; and you must have one man of that sort to say the things that nobody else will say.

THE COUNT. It seems to me to carry the principle of division of labor too far, this keeping of the honesty and the other qualities in separate compartments. What is Mr Gunn's speciality, if I may ask?

SAVOYARD. Gunn is one of the intellectuals.

THE COUNT. But arnt they all intellectuals?

SAVOYARD. Lord! no: heaven forbid! You must be careful what you say about that: I shouldnt like anyone to call me an Intellectual: I dont think any Englishman would! They dont count really, you know; but still it's rather the thing to have them. Gunn is one of the young intellectuals: he writes plays himself. Hes useful because he pitches into the older intellectuals who are standing in his way. But you may take it from me that none of these chaps really matter. Flawner Bannal's your man. Bannal really represents the British playgoer. When he likes a thing, you may take your oath there are a hundred thousand people in London thatll like it if they can only be got to know about it. Besides, Bannal's knowledge of the theatre is an inside knowledge. We know him; and he knows us. He knows the ropes: he knows his way about: he knows what hes talking about.

THE COUNT. [with a little sigh] Age and experience, I suppose?

SAVOYARD. Age! I should put him at twenty at the very outside, myself. It's not an old man's job after all, is it? Bannal may not ride the literary high horse like Trotter and the rest; but I'd take his opinion before any other in London. Hes the man in the street; and thats what you want.

THE COUNT. I am almost sorry you didnt give the gentleman his full terms. I should not have grudged the fifty guineas for a sound opinion. He may feel shabbily treated.

SAVOYARD. Well, let him. It was a bit of side, his asking fifty. After all, what is he? Only a pressman. Jolly good business for him to earn ten guineas: hes done the same job often enough for half a quid, I expect.

Fanny O'Dowda comes precipitately through the

curtains, excited and nervous. A girl of nineteen in a dress synchronous with her father's.

FANNY. Papa, papa, the critics have come. And one of them has a cocked hat and sword like a - [she notices Savoyard] Oh, I beg your pardon.

THE COUNT. This is Mr Savoyard, your impresario, my dear.

FANNY. [shaking hands] How do you do?

SAVOYARD. Pleased to meet you, Miss O'Dowda. The cocked hat is all right. Trotter is a member of the new Academic Committee. He induced them to go in for a uniform like the French Academy; and I asked him to wear it.

THE FOOTMAN. [announcing] Mr Trotter, Mr Vaughan, Mr Gunn, Mr Flawner Bannal. [The four critics enter. Trotter wears a diplomatic dress, with sword and three-cornered hat. His age is about 50. Vaughan is 40. Gunn is 30. Flawner Bannal is 20 and is quite unlike the others. They can be classed at sight as professional men: Bannal is obviously one of those unemployables of the business class who manage to pick up a living by a sort of courage which gives him cheerfulness, conviviality, and bounce, and is helped out positively by a slight turn for writing, and negatively by a comfortable ignorance and lack of intuition which hides from him all the dangers and disgraces that keep men of finer perception in check. The Count approaches them hospitably].

SAVOYARD. Count O'Dowda, gentlemen. Mr Trotter.

TROTTER. [looking at the Count's costume] Have I the pleasure of meeting a confrere?

THE COUNT. No, sir: I have no right to my costume except the right of a lover of the arts to dress myself handsomely. You are most welcome, Mr Trotter. [Trotter bows in the French manner].

SAVOYARD. Mr Vaughan.

THE COUNT. How do you do, Mr Vaughan?

VAUGHAN. Quite well, thanks.

SAVOYARD. Mr Gunn.

THE COUNT. Delighted to make your acquaintance, Mr Gunn.

GUNN. Very pleased.

SAVOYARD. Mr Flawner Bannal.

THE COUNT. Very kind of you to come, Mr Bannal.

BANNAL. Dont mention it.

THE COUNT. Gentlemen, my daughter. [They all bow]. We are very greatly indebted to you, gentlemen, for so kindly indulging her whim. [The dressing bell sounds. The Count looks at his watch]. Ah! The dressing bell, gentlemen. As our play begins at nine, I have had to put forward the dinner hour a little. May I shew you to your rooms? [He goes out, followed by all the men, except Trotter, who, going last, is detained by Fanny].

FANNY. Mr Trotter: I want to say something to you about this play.

TROTTER. No: thats forbidden. You must not attempt to souffler the critic.

FANNY. Oh, I would not for the world try to influence your opinion.

TROTTER. But you do: you are influencing me very shockingly. You invite me to this charming house, where I'm about to enjoy a charming dinner. And just before the dinner I'm taken aside by a charming young lady to be talked to about the play. How can you expect me to be impartial? God forbid that I should set up to be a judge, or do more than record an impression; but my impressions can be influenced; and in this case youre influencing them shamelessly all the time.

FANNY. Dont make me more nervous than I am already, Mr Trotter. If you knew how I feel!

TROTTER. Naturally: your first party: your first appearance in England as hostess. But youre doing it beautifully. Dont be afraid. Every nuance is perfect.

FANNY. It's so kind of you to say so, Mr Trotter. But that isnt whats the matter. The truth is, this play is going to give my father a dreadful shock.

TROTTER. Nothing unusual in that, I'm sorry to say. Half the young ladies in London spend their evenings making their fathers take them to plays that are not fit for elderly people to see.

FANNY. Oh, I know all about that; but you cant

understand what it means to Papa. Youre not so innocent as he is.

TROTTER. [remonstrating] My dear young lady -

FANNY. I dont mean morally innocent: everybody who reads your articles knows youre as innocent as a lamb.

TROTTER. What!

FANNY. Yes, Mr Trotter: Ive seen a good deal of life since I came to England; and I assure you that to me youre a mere baby: a dear, good, well-meaning, delightful, witty, charming baby; but still just a wee lamb in a world of wolves. Cambridge is not what it was in my father's time.

TROTTER. Well, I must say!

FANNY. Just so. Thats one of our classifications in the Cambridge Fabian Society.

TROTTER. Classifications? I dont understand.

FANNY. We classify our aunts into different sorts. And one of the sorts is the "I must says."

TROTTER. I withdraw "I must say." I substitute "Blame my cats!" No: I substitute "Blame my kittens!" Observe, Miss O'Dowda: kittens. I say again in the teeth of the whole Cambridge Fabian Society, kittens. Impertinent little kittens. Blame them. Smack them. I guess what is on your conscience. This play to which you have lured me is one of those in which members of Fabian Societies instruct their grandmothers in the art of milking ducks. And you are afraid it will shock your father. Well, I hope it will. And if he consults me about it I shall recommend him to smack you soundly and pack you off to bed.

FANNY. Thats one of your prettiest literary attitudes, Mr Trotter; but it doesnt take me in. You see, I'm much more conscious of what you really are than you are yourself, because weve discussed you thoroughly at Cambridge; and youve never discussed yourself, have you?

TROTTER. I -

FANNY. Of course you havnt; so you see it's no good Trottering at me.

TROTTER. Trottering!

FANNY. Thats what we call it at Cambridge.

TROTTER. If it were not so obviously a stage cliche, I should say Damn Cambridge. As it is, I blame my kittens. And now let me warn you. If youre going to be a charming healthy young English girl, you may coax me. If youre going to be an unsexed Cambridge Fabian virago, I'll treat you as my intellectual equal, as I would treat a man.

FANNY. [adoringly] But how few men are your intellectual equals, Mr Trotter!

TROTTER. I'm getting the worst of this.

FANNY. Oh no. Why do you say that?

TROTTER. May I remind you that the dinner-bell will ring presently?

FANNY. What does it matter? We're both ready. I havnt told you yet what I want you to do for me.

TROTTER. Nor have you particularly predisposed me to do it, except out of pure magnanimity. What is it?

FANNY. I dont mind this play shocking my father morally. It's good for him to be shocked morally. It's all that the young can do for the old, to shock them and keep them up to date. But I know that this play will shock him artistically; and that terrifies me. No moral consideration could make a breach between us: he would forgive me for anything of that kind sooner or later; but he never gives way on a point of art. I darent let him know that I love Beethoven and Wagner; and as to Strauss, if he heard three bars of Elektra, it'd part us for ever. Now what I want you to do is this. If hes very angry - if he hates the play, because it's a modern play - will you tell him that it's not my fault; that its style and construction, and so forth, are considered the very highest art nowadays; that the author wrote it in the proper way for repertory theatres of the most superior kind - you know the kind of plays I mean?

TROTTER. [emphatically] I think I know the sort of entertainments you mean. But please do not beg a vital question by calling them plays. I dont pretend to be an authority; but I have at least established the fact that these productions, whatever else they may be, are certainly not plays.

FANNY. The authors dont say they are.

TROTTER. [warmly] I am aware that one author, who is, I blush to say, a personal friend of mine, resorts freely to the dastardly subterfuge of calling them conversations, discussions, and so forth, with the express object of evading criticism. But I'm not to be disarmed by such tricks. I say they are not plays. Dialogues, if you will. Exhibitions of character, perhaps: especially the character of the author. Fictions, possibly, though a little decent reticence as to introducing actual persons, and thus violating the sanctity of private life, might not be amiss. But plays, no. I say NO. Not plays. If you will not concede this point I cant continue our conversation. I take this seriously. It's a matter of principle. I must ask you, Miss O'Dowda, before we go a step further, Do you or do you not claim that these works are plays?

FANNY. I assure you I dont.

TROTTER. Not in any sense of the word?

FANNY. Not in any sense of the word. I loathe plays.

TROTTER. [disappointed] That last remark destroys all the value of your admission. You admire these - these theatrical nondescripts? You enjoy them?

FANNY. Dont you?

TROTTER. Of course I do. Do you take me for a fool? Do you suppose I prefer popular melodramas? Have I not written most appreciative notices of them? But I say theyre not plays. Theyre not plays. I cant consent to remain in this house another minute if anything remotely resembling them is to be foisted on me as a play.

FANNY. I fully admit that theyre not plays. I only want you to tell my father that plays are not plays nowadays - not in your sense of the word.

TROTTER. Ah, there you go again! In my sense of the word! You believe that my criticism is merely a personal impression; that -

FANNY. You always said it was.

TROTTER. Pardon me: not on this point. If you had been classically educated -

FANNY. But I have.

TROTTER. Pooh! Cambridge! If you had been educated at Oxford, you would know that the definition of a play has been settled exactly and scientifically for two thousand two hundred and sixty years. When I say that these entertainments are not plays, I dont mean in my sense of the word, but in the sense given to it for all time by the immortal Stagirite.

FANNY. Who is the Stagirite?

TROTTER. [shocked] You dont know who the Stagirite was?

FANNY. Sorry. Never heard of him.

TROTTER. And this is Cambridge education! Well, my dear young lady, I'm delighted to find theres something you don't know; and I shant spoil you by dispelling an ignorance which, in my opinion, is highly becoming to your age and sex. So we'll leave it at that.

FANNY. But you will promise to tell my father that lots of people write plays just like this one - that I havnt selected it out of mere heartlessness?

TROTTER. I cant possibly tell you what I shall say to your father about the play until Ive seen the play. But I'll tell you what I shall say to him about you. I shall say that youre a very foolish young lady; that youve got into a very questionable set; and that the sooner he takes you away from Cambridge and its Fabian Society, the better.

FANNY. It's so funny to hear you pretending to be a heavy father. In Cambridge we regard you as a bel esprit, a wit, an Irresponsible, a Parisian Immoralist, tres chic.

TROTTER. I!

FANNY. Theres quite a Trotter set.

TROTTER. Well, upon my word!

FANNY. They go in for adventures and call you Aramis.

TROTTER. They wouldnt dare!

FANNY. You always make such delicious fun of the serious people. Your insouciance -

TROTTER. [frantic] Stop talking French to me: it's not a proper language for a young girl. Great heavens! how is it possible that a few innocent pleasantries should be so frightfully misunderstood? Ive tried all my life to be sincere and simple, to be unassuming and kindly. Ive lived a blameless life. Ive supported the Censorship in the face of ridicule and insult. And now I'm told that I'm a centre of Immoralism! of Modern Minxism! a trifler with the most sacred subjects! a Nietzschean!! perhaps a Shavian!!!

FANNY. Do you mean you are really on the serious side, Mr Trotter?

TROTTER. Of course I'm on the serious side. How dare you ask me such a question?

FANNY. Then why dont you play for it?

TROTTER. I do play for it - short, of course, of making myself ridiculous.

FANNY. What! not make yourself ridiculous for the sake of a good cause! Oh, Mr Trotter. Thats vieux jeu.

TROTTER. [shouting at her] Dont talk French. I will not allow it.

FANNY. But this dread of ridicule is so frightfully out of date. The Cambridge Fabian Society -

TROTTER. I forbid you to mention the Fabian Society to me.

FANNY. Its motto is "You cannot learn to skate without making yourself ridiculous."

TROTTER. Skate! What has that to do with it?

FANNY. Thats not all. It goes on, "The ice of life is slippery."

TROTTER. Ice of life indeed! You should be eating penny ices and enjoying yourself. I wont hear another word.

The Count returns.

THE COUNT. We're all waiting in the drawing-room, my dear. Have you been detaining Mr Trotter all this time?

TROTTER. I'm so sorry. I must have just a little brush up: I [He hurries out].

THE COUNT. My dear, you should be in the drawing-room. You should not have kept him here.

FANNY. I know. Dont scold me: I had something important to say to him.

THE COUNT. I shall ask him to take you in to dinner.

FANNY. Yes, papa. Oh, I hope it will go off well.

THE COUNT. Yes, love, of course it will. Come along.

FANNY. Just one thing, papa, whilst we're alone. Who was the Stagirite?

THE COUNT. The Stagirite? Do you mean to say you dont know?

FANNY. Havnt the least notion.

THE COUNT. The Stagirite was Aristotle. By the way,

dont mention him to Mr Trotter.

They go to the dining-room.

THE PLAY

ACT I

In the dining-room of a house in Denmark Hill, an elderly lady sits at breakfast reading the newspaper. Her chair is at the end of the oblong dining-table furthest from the fire. There is an empty chair at the other end. The fireplace is behind this chair; and the door is next the fireplace, between it and the corner. An arm-chair stands beside the coal-scuttle. In the middle of the back wall is the sideboard, parallel to the table. The rest of the furniture is mostly dining-room chairs, ranged against the walls, and including a baby rocking-chair on the lady's side of the room. The lady is a placid person. Her husband, Mr Robin Gilbey, not at all placid, bursts violently into the room with a letter in his hand.

GILBEY. [grinding his teeth] This is a nice thing. This is a b -

MRS GILBEY. [cutting him short] Leave it at that, please. Whatever it is, bad language wont make it better.

GILBEY. [bitterly] Yes, put me in the wrong as usual. Take your boy's part against me. [He flings himself into the empty chair opposite her].

MRS GILBEY. When he does anything right, hes your son. When he does anything wrong hes mine. Have you any news of him?

GILBEY. Ive a good mind not to tell you.

MRS GILBEY. Then dont. I suppose hes been found. Thats a comfort, at all events.

GILBEY. No, he hasnt been found. The boy may be at the bottom of the river for all you care. [Too agitated to sit quietly, he rises and paces the room distractedly].

MRS GILBEY. Then what have you got in your hand?

GILBEY. Ive a letter from the Monsignor Grenfell. From New York. Dropping us. Cutting us. [Turning fiercely on her] Thats a nice thing, isnt it?

MRS GILBEY. What for?

GILBEY. [flinging away towards his chair] How do I know what for?

MRS GILBEY. What does he say?

GILBEY. [sitting down and grumblingly adjusting his spectacles] This is what he says. "My dear Mr Gilbey: The news about Bobby had to follow me across the Atlantic: it did not reach me until to-day. I am afraid he is incorrigible. My brother, as you may imagine, feels that this last escapade has gone beyond the bounds; and I think, myself, that Bobby ought to be made to feel that such scrapes involve a certain degree of reprobation." "As you may imagine"! And we know no more about it than the babe unborn.

MRS GILBEY. What else does he say?

GILBEY. "I think my brother must have been just a little to blame himself; so, between ourselves, I shall, with due and impressive formality, forgive Bobby later on; but for the present I think it had better be understood that he is in disgrace, and that we are no longer on visiting terms. As ever, yours sincerely." [His agitation masters him again] Thats a nice slap in the face to get from a man in his position! This is what your son has brought on me.

MRS GILBEY. Well, I think it's rather a nice letter. He as good as tells you hes only letting on to be offended for Bobby's good.

GILBEY. Oh, very well: have the letter framed and hang it up over the mantelpiece as a testimonial.

MRS GILBEY. Dont talk nonsense, Rob. You ought to be thankful to know that the boy is alive after his disappearing like that for nearly a week.

GILBEY. Nearly a week! A fortnight, you mean. Wheres your feelings, woman? It was fourteen days yesterday.

MRS GILBEY. Oh, dont call it fourteen days, Rob, as if the boy was in prison.

GILBEY. How do you know hes not in prison? It's got

on my nerves so, that I'd believe even that.

MRS GILBEY. Dont talk silly, Rob. Bobby might get into a scrape like any other lad; but he'd never do anything low.

Juggins, the footman, comes in with a card on a salver. He is a rather low-spirited man of thirty-five or more, of good appearance and address, and iron self-command.

JUGGINS. [presenting the salver to Mr Gilbey] Lady wishes to see Mr Bobby's parents, sir.

GILBEY. [pointing to Mrs Gilbey] Theres Mr Bobby's parent. I disown him.

JUGGINS. Yes, sir. [He presents the salver to Mrs Gilbey].

MRS GILBEY. You mustnt mind what your master says, Juggins: he doesnt mean it. [She takes the card and reads it]. Well, I never!

GILBEY. Whats up now?

MRS GILBEY. [reading] "Miss D. Delaney. Darling Dora." Just like that - in brackets. What sort of person, Juggins?

GILBEY. Whats her address?

MRS GILBEY. The West Circular Road. Is that a respectable address, Juggins?

JUGGINS. A great many most respectable people live

in the West Circular Road, madam; but the address is not a guarantee of respectability.

GILBEY. So it's come to that with him, has it?

MRS GILBEY. Dont jump to conclusions, Rob. How do you know? [To Juggins] Is she a lady, Juggins? You know what I mean.

JUGGINS. In the sense in which you are using the word, no, madam.

MRS GILBEY. I'd better try what I can get out of her. [To Juggins] Shew her up. You dont mind, do you, Rob?

GILBEY. So long as you dont flounce out and leave me alone with her. [He rises and plants himself on the hearth-rug].

Juggins goes out.

MRS GILBEY. I wonder what she wants, Rob?

GILBEY. If she wants money, she shant have it. Not a farthing. A nice thing, everybody seeing her on our doorstep! If it wasnt that she may tell us something about the lad, I'd have Juggins put the hussy into the street.

JUGGINS. [returning and announcing] Miss Delaney. [He waits for express orders before placing a chair for this visitor].

Miss Delaney comes in. She is a young lady of hilarious disposition, very tolerable good looks, and killing clothes. She is so affable and confidential that it is very difficult to keep her at a distance by any process short of flinging her out of the house.

DORA. [plunging at once into privileged intimacy and into the middle of the room] How d'ye do, both. I'm a friend of Bobby's. He told me all about you once, in a moment of confidence. Of course he never let on who he was at the police court.

GILBEY. Police court!

MRS GILBEY. [looking apprehensively at Juggins] Tch - ! Juggins: a chair.

DORA. Oh, Ive let it out, have I! [Contemplating Juggins approvingly as he places a chair for her between the table and the sideboard] But hes the right sort: I can see that. [Buttonholing him] You wont let on downstairs, old man, will you?

JUGGINS. The family can rely on my absolute discretion. [He withdraws].

DORA. [sitting down genteelly] I dont know what youll say to me: you know I really have no right to come here; but then what was I to do? You know Holy Joe, Bobby's tutor, dont you? But of course you do.

GILBEY. [with dignity] I know Mr Joseph Grenfell, the brother of Monsignor Grenfell, if it is of him you are speaking.

DORA. [wide-eyed and much amused] No!!! You dont tell me that old geezer has a brother a Monsignor! And youre Catholics! And I never knew it, though Ive known Bobby ever so long! But of course the last thing you find out about a person is their religion, isnt it?

MRS GILBEY. We're not Catholics. But when the Samuelses got an Archdeacon's son to form their boy's mind, Mr Gilbey thought Bobby ought to have a chance too. And the Monsignor is a customer. Mr Gilbey consulted him about Bobby; and he recommended a brother of his that was more sinned against than sinning.

GILBEY. [on tenderhooks] She dont want to hear about that, Maria. [To Dora] Whats your business?

DORA. I'm afraid it was all my fault.

GILBEY. What was all your fault? I'm half distracted. I dont know what has happened to the boy: hes been lost these fourteen days -

MRS GILBEY. A fortnight, Rob.

GILBEY. - and not a word have we heard of him since.

MRS GILBEY. Dont fuss, Rob.

GILBEY. [yelling] I will fuss. Youve no feeling. You dont care what becomes of the lad. [He sits down savagely].

DORA. [soothingly] Youve been anxious about him. Of course. How thoughtless of me not to begin by telling you hes quite safe. Indeed hes in the safest place in the world, as one may say: safe under lock and key.

GILBEY. [horrified, pitiable] Oh my - [his breath fails him]. Do you mean that when he was in the police court he was in the dock? Oh, Maria! Oh, great Lord! What has he done? What has he got for it? [Desperate] Will you tell me or will you see me go mad on my own carpet?

DORA. [sweetly] Yes, old dear -

MRS GILBEY. [starting at the familiarity] Well!

DORA. [continuing] I'll tell you: but dont you worry: hes all right. I came out myself this morning: there was such a crowd! and a band! they thought I was a suffragette: only fancy! You see it was like this. Holy Joe got talking about how he'd been a champion sprinter at college.

MRS GILBEY. A what?

DORA. A sprinter. He said he was the fastest hundred yards runner in England. We were all in the old cowshed that night.

MRS GILBEY. What old cowshed?

GILBEY. [groaning] Oh, get on. Get on.

DORA. Oh, of course you wouldnt know. How silly of me! It's a rather go-ahead sort of music hall in Stepney. We call it the old cowshed.

MRS GILBEY. Does Mr Grenfell take Bobby to music halls?

DORA. No. Bobby takes him. But Holy Joe likes it:

fairly laps it up like a kitten, poor old dear. Well, Bobby says to me, "Darling - "

MRS GILBEY. [placidly] Why does he call you Darling?

DORA. Oh, everybody calls me Darling: it's a sort of name Ive got. Darling Dora, you know. Well, he says, "Darling, if you can get Holy Joe to sprint a hundred yards, I'll stand you that squiffer with the gold keys."

MRS GILBEY. Does he call his tutor Holy Joe to his face [Gilbey clutches at his hair in his impatience].

DORA. Well, what would he call him? After all, Holy Joe is Holy Joe; and boys will be boys.

MRS GILBEY. Whats a squiffer?

DORA. Oh, of course: excuse my vulgarity: a concertina. Theres one in a shop in Green Street, ivory inlaid, with gold keys and Russia leather bellows; and Bobby knew I hankered after it; but he couldn't afford it, poor lad, though I knew he just longed to give it to me.

GILBEY. Maria: if you keep interrupting with silly questions, I shall go out of my senses. Heres the boy in gaol and me disgraced for ever; and all you care to know is what a squiffer is.

DORA. Well, remember it has gold keys. The man wouldnt take a penny less than 15 pounds for it. It was a presentation one.

GILBEY. [shouting at her] Wheres my son? Whats

happened to my son? Will you tell me that, and stop cackling about your squiffer?

DORA. Oh, aint we impatient! Well, it does you credit, old dear. And you neednt fuss: theres no disgrace. Bobby behaved like a perfect gentleman. Besides, it was all my fault. I'll own it: I took too much champagne. I was not what you might call drunk; but I was bright, and a little beyond myself; and - I'll confess it - I wanted to shew off before Bobby, because he was a bit taken by a woman on the stage; and she was pretending to be game for anything. You see you've brought Bobby up too strict; and when he gets loose theres no holding him. He does enjoy life more than any lad I ever met.

GILBEY. Never you mind how hes been brought up: thats my business. Tell me how hes been brought down: thats yours.

MRS GILBEY. Oh, dont be rude to the lady, Rob.

DORA. I'm coming to it, old dear: dont you be so headstrong. Well, it was a beautiful moonlight night; and we couldnt get a cab on the nod; so we started to walk, very jolly, you know: arm in arm, and dancing along, singing and all that. When we came into Jamaica Square, there was a young copper on point duty at the corner. I says to Bob: "Dearie boy: is it a bargain about the squiffer if I make Joe sprint for you?" "Anything you like, darling," says he: "I love you." I put on my best company manners and stepped up to the copper. "If you please, sir," says I, "can you direct me to Carrickmines Square?" I was so genteel, and talked so sweet, that he fell to it like a bird. "I never heard of any such Square in these parts," he says.

"Then," says I, "what a very silly little officer you must be!"; and I gave his helmet a chuck behind that knocked it over his eyes, and did a bunk.

MRS GILBEY. Did a what?

DORA. A bunk. Holy Joe did one too all right: he sprinted faster than he ever did in college, I bet, the old dear. He got clean off, too. Just as he was overtaking me half-way down the square, we heard the whistle; and at the sound of it he drew away like a streak of lightning; and that was the last I saw of him. I was copped in the Dock Road myself: rotten luck, wasn't it? I tried the innocent and genteel and all the rest; but Bobby's hat done me in.

GILBEY. And what happened to the boy?

DORA. Only fancy! he stopped to laugh at the copper! He thought the copper would see the joke, poor lamb. He was arguing about it when the two that took me came along to find out what the whistle was for, and brought me with them. Of course I swore I'd never seen him before in my life; but there he was in my hat and I in his. The cops were very spiteful and laid it on for all they were worth: drunk and disorderly and assaulting the police and all that. I got fourteen days without the option, because you see - well, the fact is, I'd done it before, and been warned. Bobby was a first offender and had the option; but the dear boy had no money left and wouldnt give you away by telling his name; and anyhow he couldnt have brought himself to buy himself off and leave me there; so hes doing his time. Well, it was two forty shillingses; and Ive only twenty-eight shillings in the world. If I pawn my clothes I shant be able to earn any more. So I cant pay the fine and get him out; but if youll stand 3 pounds I'll stand one; and thatll do it. If youd like to be very kind and nice you could pay the lot; but I cant deny that it was my fault; so I wont press you.

GILBEY. [heart-broken] My son in gaol!

DORA. Oh, cheer up, old dear: it wont hurt him: look at me after fourteen days of it; I'm all the better for being kept a bit quiet. You mustnt let it prey on your mind.

GILBEY. The disgrace of it will kill me. And it will leave a mark on him to the end of his life.

DORA. Not a bit of it. Dont you be afraid: Ive educated Bobby a bit: hes not the mollycoddle he was when you had him in hand.

MRS GILBEY. Indeed Bobby is not a mollycoddle. They wanted him to go in for singlestick at the Young Men's Christian Association; but, of course, I couldnt allow that: he might have had his eye knocked out.

GILBEY. [to Dora, angrily] Listen here, you.

DORA. Oh, aint we cross!

GILBEY. I want none of your gaiety here. This is a respectable household. Youve gone and got my poor innocent boy into trouble. It's the like of you thats the ruin of the like of him.

DORA. So you always say, you old dears. But you know better. Bobby came to me: I didnt come to him.

GILBEY. Would he have gone if you hadnt been there for him to go to? Tell me that. You know why he went to you, I suppose?

DORA. [charitably] It was dull for him at home, poor lad, wasn't it?

MRS GILBEY. Oh no. I'm at home on first Thursdays. And we have the Knoxes to dinner every Friday. Margaret Knox and Bobby are as good as engaged. Mr Knox is my husband's partner. Mrs Knox is very religious; but shes quite cheerful. We dine with them on Tuesdays. So thats two evenings pleasure every week.

GILBEY. [almost in tears] We done what we could for the boy. Short of letting him go into temptations of all sorts, he can do what he likes. What more does he want?

DORA. Well, old dear, he wants me; and thats about the long and short of it. And I must say youre not very nice to me about it. Ive talked to him like a mother, and tried my best to keep him straight; but I dont deny I like a bit of fun myself; and we both get a bit giddy when we're lighthearted. Him and me is a pair, I'm afraid.

GILBEY. Dont talk foolishness, girl. How could you and he be a pair, you being what you are, and he brought up as he has been, with the example of a religious woman like Mrs Knox before his eyes? I cant understand how he could bring himself to be seen in the street with you. [Pitying himself] I havnt deserved this. Ive done my duty as a father. Ive kept him sheltered. [Angry with her] Creatures like you that take advantage of a child's innocence ought to be whipped through the streets.

DORA. Well, whatever I may be, I'm too much the lady to lose my temper; and I dont think Bobby would like me to tell you what I think of you; for when I start giving people a bit of my mind I sometimes use language thats beneath me. But I tell you once for all I must have the money to get Bobby out; and if you wont fork out, I'll hunt up Holy Joe. He might get it off his brother, the Monsignor.

GILBEY. You mind your own concerns. My solicitor will do what is right. I'll not have you paying my son's fine as if you were anything to him.

DORA. Thats right. Youll get him out today, wont you?

GILBEY. It's likely I'd leave my boy in prison, isnt it?

DORA. I'd like to know when theyll let him out.

GILBEY. You would, would you? Youre going to meet him at the prison door.

DORA. Well, dont you think any woman would that had the feelings of a lady?

GILBEY. [bitterly] Oh yes: I know. Here! I must buy the lad's salvation, I suppose. How much will you take to clear out and let him go?

DORA. [pitying him: quite nice about it] What good would that do, old dear? There are others, you know.

GILBEY. Thats true. I must send the boy himself away.

DORA. Where to?

GILBEY. Anywhere, so long as hes out of the reach of you and your like.

DORA. Then I'm afraid youll have to send him out of the world, old dear. I'm sorry for you: I really am, though you mightnt believe it; and I think your feelings do you real credit. But I cant give him up just to let him fall into the hands of people I couldnt trust, can I?

GILBEY. [beside himself, rising] Wheres the police? Wheres the Government? Wheres the Church? Wheres respectability and right reason? Whats the good of them if I have to stand here and see you put my son in your pocket as if he was a chattel slave, and you hardly out of gaol as a common drunk and disorderly? Whats the world coming to?

DORA. It is a lottery, isnt it, old dear?

Mr Gilbey rushes from the room, distracted.

MRS GILBEY. [unruffled] Where did you buy that white lace? I want some to match a collaret of my own; and I cant get it at Perry and John's.

DORA. Knagg and Pantle's: one and fourpence. It's machine hand-made.

MRS GILBEY. I never give more than one and tuppence. But I suppose youre extravagant by nature. My sister Martha was just like that. Pay anything she was asked.

DORA. Whats tuppence to you, Mrs Bobby, after all?

MRS GILBEY. [correcting her] Mrs Gilbey.

DORA. Of course, Mrs Gilbey. I am silly.

MRS GILBEY. Bobby must have looked funny in your hat. Why did you change hats with him?

DORA. I dont know. One does, you know.

MRS GILBEY. I never did. The things people do! I cant understand them. Bobby never told me he was keeping company with you. His own mother!

DORA. [overcome] Excuse me: I cant help smiling.

Juggins enters.

JUGGINS. Mr Gilbey has gone to Wormwood Scrubbs, madam.

MRS GILBEY. Have you ever been in a police court, Juggins?

JUGGINS. Yes, madam.

MRS GILBEY [rather shocked] I hope you had not been exceeding, Juggins.

JUGGINS. Yes, madam, I had. I exceeded the legal limit.

MRS GILBEY. Oh, that! Why do they give a woman a

fortnight for wearing a man's hat, and a man a month for wearing hers?

JUGGINS. I didnt know that they did, madam.

MRS GILBEY. It doesnt seem justice, does it, Juggins?

JUGGINS. No, madam.

MRS GILBEY [to Dora, rising] Well, good-bye. [Shaking her hand] So pleased to have made your acquaintance.

DORA. [standing up] Dont mention it. I'm sure it's most kind of you to receive me at all.

MRS GILBEY. I must go off now and order lunch. [She trots to the door]. What was it you called the concertina?

DORA. A squiffer, dear.

MRS GILBEY. [thoughtfully] A squiffer, of course. How funny! [She goes out].

DORA. [exploding into ecstasies of mirth] Oh my! isnt she an old love? How do you keep your face straight?

JUGGINS. It is what I am paid for.

DORA. [confidentially] Listen here, dear boy. Your name isnt Juggins. Nobody's name is Juggins.

JUGGINS. My orders are, Miss Delaney, that you are not to be here when Mr Gilbey returns from

Wormwood Scrubbs.

DORA. That means telling me to mind my own business, doesnt it? Well, I'm off. Tootle Loo, Charlie Darling. [She kisses her hand to him and goes].

ACT II

On the afternoon of the same day, Mrs Knox is writing notes in her drawing-room, at a writing-table which stands against the wall. Anyone placed so as to see Mrs Knox's left profile, will have the door on the right and the window an the left, both further away than Mrs Knox, whose back is presented to an obsolete upright piano at the opposite side of the room. The sofa is near the piano. There is a small table in the middle of the room, with some gilt-edged books and albums on it, and chairs near it.

Mr Knox comes in almost furtively, a troubled man of fifty, thinner, harder, and uglier than his partner, Gilbey, Gilbey being a soft stoutish man with white hair and thin smooth skin, whilst Knox has coarse black hair, and blue jaws which no diligence in shaving can whiten. Mrs Knox is a plain woman, dressed without regard to fashion, with thoughtful eyes and thoughtful ways that make an atmosphere of peace and some solemnity. She is surprised to see her husband at home during business hours.

MRS KNOX. What brings you home at this hour? Have you heard anything?

KNOX. No. Have you?

MRS KNOX. No. Whats the matter?

KNOX. [sitting down on the sofa] I believe Gilbey has found out.

MRS KNOX. What makes you think that?

KNOX. Well, I dont know: I didnt like to tell you: you have enough to worry you without that; but Gilbey's been very queer ever since it happened. I cant keep my mind on business as I ought; and I was depending on him. But hes worse than me. Hes not looking after anything; and he keeps out of my way. His manner's not natural. He hasnt asked us to dinner; and hes never said a word about our not asking him to dinner, after all these years when weve dined every week as regular as clockwork. It looks to me as if Gilbey's trying to drop me socially. Well, why should he do that if he hasnt heard?

MRS KNOX. I wonder! Bobby hasnt been near us either: thats what I cant make out.

KNOX. Oh, thats nothing. I told him Margaret was down in Cornwall with her aunt.

MRS KNOX. [reproachfully] Jo! [She takes her handkerchief from the writing-table and cries a little].

KNOX. Well, I got to tell lies, aint I? You wont. Somebody's got to tell em.

MRS KNOX. [putting away her handkerchief] It only ends in our not knowing what to believe. Mrs Gilbey told me Bobby was in Brighton for the sea air. Theres something queer about that. Gilbey would never let the boy loose by himself among the temptations of a gay place like Brighton without his tutor; and I saw the tutor in Kensington High Street the very day she told me.

KNOX. If the Gilbeys have found out, it's all over between Bobby and Margaret, and all over between us and them.

MRS KNOX. It's all over between us and everybody. When a girl runs away from home like that, people know what to think of her and her parents.

KNOX. She had a happy, respectable home - everything -

MRS KNOX. [interrupting him] Theres no use going over it all again, Jo. If a girl hasnt happiness in herself, she wont be happy anywhere. Youd better go back to the shop and try to keep your mind off it.

KNOX. [rising restlessly] I cant. I keep fancying everybody knows it and is sniggering about it. I'm at peace nowhere but here. It's a comfort to be with you. It's a torment to be with other people.

MRS KNOX. [going to him and drawing her arm through his] There, Jo, there! I'm sure I'd have you here always if I could. But it cant be. God's work must go on from day to day, no matter what comes. We must face our trouble and bear it.

KNOX. [wandering to the window arm in arm with her] Just look at the people in the street, going up and down as if nothing had happened. It seems unnatural, as if they all knew and didnt care.

MRS KNOX. If they knew, Jo, thered be a crowd round the house looking up at us. You shouldnt keep thinking about it.

KNOX. I know I shouldnt. You have your religion, Amelia; and I'm sure I'm glad it comforts you. But it doesnt come to me that way. Ive worked hard to get a position and be respectable. Ive turned many a girl out of the shop for being half an hour late at night; and heres my own daughter gone for a fortnight without word or sign, except a telegram to say shes not dead and that we're not to worry about her.

MRS KNOX. [suddenly pointing to the street] Jo, look!

KNOX. Margaret! With a man!

MRS KNOX. Run down, Jo, quick. Catch her: save her.

KNOX. [lingering] Shes shaking bands with him: shes coming across to the door.

MRS KNOX. [energetically] Do as I tell you. Catch the man before hes out of sight.

Knox rushes from the room. Mrs Knox looks anxiously and excitedly from the window. Then she throws up the sash and leans out. Margaret Knox comes in, flustered and annoyed. She is a strong, springy girl of eighteen, with large nostrils, an audacious chin, and a gaily resolute manner, even peremptory on occasions like the present, when she is annoyed.

MARGARET. Mother. Mother.

Mrs Knox draws in her head and confronts her daughter.

MRS KNOX. [sternly] Well, miss?

MARGARET. Oh, mother, do go out and stop father making a scene in the street. He rushed at him and said "Youre the man who took away my daughter" loud enough for all the people to hear. Everybody stopped. We shall have a crowd round the house. Do do something to stop him.

Knox returns with a good-looking young marine officer.

MARGARET. Oh, Monsieur Duvallet, I'm so sorry - so ashamed. Mother: this is Monsieur Duvallet, who has been extremely kind to me. Monsieur Duvallet: my mother. [Duvallet bows].

KNOX. A Frenchman! It only needed this.

MARGARET. [much annoyed] Father: do please be commonly civil to a gentleman who has been of the greatest service to me. What will he think of us?

DUVALLET. [debonair] But it's very natural. I understand Mr Knox's feelings perfectly. [He speaks English better than Knox, having learnt it on both sides of the Atlantic].

KNOX. If Ive made any mistake I'm ready to apologize. But I want to know where my daughter has been for the last fortnight.

DUVALLET. She has been, I assure you, in a

particularly safe place.

KNOX. Will you tell me what place? I can judge for myself how safe it was.

MARGARET. Holloway Gaol. Was that safe enough?

KNOX AND MRS KNOX. Holloway Gaol!

KNOX. Youve joined the Suffragets!

MARGARET. No. I wish I had. I could have had the same experience in better company. Please sit down, Monsieur Duvallet. [She sits between the table and the sofa. Mrs Knox, overwhelmed, sits at the other side of the table. Knox remains standing in the middle of the room].

DUVALLET. [sitting down on the sofa] It was nothing. An adventure. Nothing.

MARGARET. [obdurately] Drunk and assaulting the police! Forty shillings or a month!

MRS KNOX. Margaret! Who accused you of such a thing?

MARGARET. The policeman I assaulted.

KNOX. You mean to say that you did it!

MARGARET. I did. I had that satisfaction at all events. I knocked two of his teeth out.

KNOX. And you sit there coolly and tell me this!

MARGARET. Well, where do you want me to sit? Whats the use of saying things like that?

KNOX. My daughter in Holloway Gaol!

MARGARET. All the women in Holloway are somebody's daughters. Really, father, you must make up your mind to it. If you had sat in that cell for fourteen days making up your mind to it, you would understand that I'm not in the humor to be gaped at while youre trying to persuade yourself that it cant be real. These things really do happen to real people every day; and you read about them in the papers and think it's all right. Well, theyve happened to me: thats all.

KNOX. [feeble-forcible] But they shouldnt have happened to you. Dont you know that?

MARGARET. They shouldnt happen to anybody, I suppose. But they do. [Rising impatiently] And really I'd rather go out and assault another policeman and go back to Holloway than keep talking round and round it like this. If youre going to turn me out of the house, turn me out: the sooner I go the better.

DUVALLET. [rising quickly] That is impossible, mademoiselle. Your father has his position to consider. To turn his daughter out of doors would ruin him socially.

KNOX. Oh, youve put her up to that, have you? And where did you come in, may I ask?

DUVALLET. I came in at your invitation - at your amiable insistence, in fact, not at my own. But you need have no anxiety on my account. I was concerned in the regrettable incident which led to your daughter's incarceration. I got a fortnight without the option of a fine on the ridiculous ground that I ought to have struck the policeman with my fist. I should have done so with pleasure had I known; but, as it was, I struck him on the ear with my boot - a magnificent moulinet, I must say - and was informed that I had been guilty of an act of cowardice, but that for the sake of the ententecordiale I should be dealt with leniently. Yet Miss Knox, who used her fist, got a month, but with the option of a fine. I did not know this until I was released, when my first act was to pay the fine. And here we are.

MRS KNOX. You ought to pay the gentleman the fine, Jo.

KNOX. [reddening] Oh, certainly. [He takes out some money].

DUVALLET. Oh please! it does not matter. [Knox hands him two sovereigns]. If you insist - [he pockets them] Thank you.

MARGARET. I'm ever so much obliged to you, Monsieur Duvallet.

DUVALLET. Can I be of any further assistance, mademoiselle?

MARGARET. I think you had better leave us to fight it out, if you dont mind.

DUVALLET. Perfectly. Madame [bow] - Mademoiselle [bow] – Monsieur [bow] - [He goes out].

MRS KNOX. Dont ring, Jo. See the gentleman out yourself.

Knox hastily sees Duvallet out. Mother and daughter sit looking forlornly at one another without saying a word. Mrs Knox slowly sits down. Margaret follows her example. They look at one another again. Mr Knox returns.

KNOX. [shortly and sternly] Amelia: this is your job. [To Margaret] I leave you to your mother. I shall have my own say in the matter when I hear what you have to say to her. [He goes out, solemn and offended].

MARGARET. [with a bitter little laugh] Just what the Suffraget said to me in Holloway. He throws the job on you.

MRS KNOX. [reproachfully] Margaret!

MARGARET. You know it's true.

MRS KNOX. Margaret: if youre going to be hardened about it, theres no use my saying anything.

MARGARET. I'm not hardened, mother. But I cant talk nonsense about it. You see, it's all real to me. Ive suffered it. Ive been shoved and bullied. Ive had my arms twisted. Ive been made scream with pain in other ways. Ive been flung into a filthy cell with a lot of other poor wretches as if I were a sack of coals being emptied into a cellar. And the only difference between me and the others was that I hit back. Yes I did. And I did worse. I wasnt ladylike. I cursed. I called names. I heard words that I didnt even know that I knew, coming out of my mouth just as if somebody else had spoken them. The policeman repeated them in court. The magistrate said he could hardly believe it. The policeman held out his hand with his two teeth in it that I knocked out. I said it was all right; that I had heard myself using those words quite distinctly; and that I had taken the good conduct prize for three years running at school. The poor old gentleman put me back for the missionary to find out who I was, and to ascertain the state of my mind. I wouldnt tell, of course, for your sakes at home here; and I wouldnt say I was sorry, or apologize to the policeman, or compensate him or anything of that sort. I wasnt sorry. The one thing that gave me any satisfaction was getting in that smack on his mouth; and I said so. So the missionary reported that I seemed hardened and that no doubt I would tell who I was after a day in prison. Then I was sentenced. So now you see I'm not a bit the sort of girl you thought me. I'm not a bit the sort of girl I thought myself. And I dont know what sort of person you really are, or what sort of person father really is. I wonder what he would say or do if he had an angry brute of a policeman twisting his arm with one hand and rushing him along by the nape of his neck with the other. He couldnt whirl his leg like a windmill and knock a policeman down by a glorious kick on the helmet. Oh, if theyd all fought as we two fought we'd have beaten them.

MRS KNOX. But how did it all begin?

MARGARET. Oh, I dont know. It was boat-race night, they said.

MRS KNOX. Boat-race night! But what had you to do with the boat race? You went to the great Salvation Festival at the Albert Hall with your aunt. She put you into the bus that passes the door. What made you get out of the bus?

MARGARET. I dont know. The meeting got on my nerves, somehow. It was the singing, I suppose: you know I love singing a good swinging hymn; and I felt it was ridiculous to go home in the bus after we had been singing so wonderfully about climbing up the golden stairs to heaven. I wanted more music - more happiness - more life. I wanted some comrade who felt as I did. I felt exalted: it seemed mean to be afraid of anything: after all, what could anyone do to me against my will? I suppose I was a little mad: at all events, I got out of the bus at Piccadilly Circus, because there was a lot of light and excitement there. I walked to Leicester Square; and went into a great theatre.

MRS KNOX. [horrified] A theatre!

MARGARET. Yes. Lots of other women were going in alone. I had to pay five shillings.

MRS KNOX. [aghast] Five shillings!

MARGARET. [apologetically] It was a lot. It was very stuffy; and I didnt like the people much, because they didnt seem to be enjoying themselves; but the stage was splendid and the music lovely. I saw that Frenchman, Monsieur Duvallet, standing against a barrier, smoking a cigarette. He seemed quite happy; and he was nice and sailorlike. I went and stood beside him, hoping he would speak to me.

MRS KNOX. [gasps] Margaret!

MARGARET. [continuing] He did, just as if he had

known me for years. We got on together like old friends. He asked me would I have some champagne; and I said it would cost too much, but that I would give anything for a dance. I longed to join the people on the stage and dance with them: one of them was the most beautiful dancer I ever saw. He told me he had come there to see her, and that when it was over we could go somewhere where there was dancing. So we went to a place where there was a band in a gallery and the floor cleared for dancing. Very few people danced: the women only wanted to shew off their dresses; but we danced and danced until a lot of them joined in. We got quite reckless; and we had champagne after all. I never enjoyed anything so much. But at last it got spoilt by the Oxford and Cambridge students up for the boat race. They got drunk; and they began to smash things; and the police came in. Then it was quite horrible. The students fought with the police; and the police suddenly got quite brutal, and began to throw everybody downstairs. They attacked the women, who were not doing anything, and treated them just as roughly as they had treated the students. Duvallet got indignant and remonstrated with a policeman, who was shoving a woman though she was going quietly as fast as she could. The policeman flung the woman through the door and then turned on Duvallet. It was then that Duvallet swung his leg like a windmill and knocked the policeman down. And then three policemen rushed at him and carried him out by the arms and legs face downwards. Two more attacked me and gave me a shove to the door. That quite maddened me. I just got in one good bang on the mouth of one of them. All the rest was dreadful. I was rushed through the streets to the police station. They kicked me with their knees; they twisted my arms; they taunted and insulted me; they called me vile names; and I told them what I thought of them, and provoked them to do their worst. Theres one good thing about being hard hurt: it makes you sleep. I slept in that filthy cell with all the other drunks sounder than I should have slept at home. I cant describe how I felt next morning: it was hideous; but the police were quite jolly; and everybody said it was a bit of English fun, and talked about last year's boat-race night when it had been a great deal worse. I was black and blue and sick and wretched. But the strange thing was that I wasnt sorry; and I'm not sorry. And I dont feel that I did anything wrong, really. [She rises and stretches her arms with a large liberating breath] Now that it's all over I'm rather proud of it; though I know now that I'm not a lady; but whether that's because we're only shopkeepers, or because nobody's really a lady except when theyre treated like ladies, I dont know. [She throws herself into a corner of the sofa].

MRS KNOX. [lost in wonder] But how could you bring yourself to do it, Margaret? I'm not blaming you: I only want to know. How could you bring yourself to do it?

MARGARET. I cant tell you. I dont understand it myself. The prayer meeting set me free, somehow. I should never have done it if it were not for the prayer meeting.

MRS KNOX. [deeply horrified] Oh, dont say such a thing as that. I know that prayer can set us free; though you could never understand me when I told you so; but it sets us free for good, not for evil.

MARGARET. Then I suppose what I did was not evil; or else I was set free for evil as well as good. As father says, you cant have anything both ways at once. When I was at home and at school I was what you call good; but I wasnt free. And when I got free I was what most people would call not good. But I see no harm in what I did; though I see plenty in what other people did to me.

MRS KNOX. I hope you dont think yourself a heroine of romance.

MARGARET. Oh no. [She sits down again at the table]. I'm a heroine of reality, if you can call me a heroine at all. And reality is pretty brutal, pretty filthy, when you come to grips with it. Yet it's glorious all the same. It's so real and satisfactory.

MRS KNOX. I dont like this spirit in you, Margaret. I dont like your talking to me in that tone.

MARGARET. It's no use, mother. I dont care for you and Papa any the less; but I shall never get back to the old way of talking again. Ive made a sort of descent into hell -

MRS KNOX. Margaret! Such a word!

MARGARET. You should have heard all the words that were flying round that night. You should mix a little with people who dont know any other words. But when I said that about a descent into hell I was not swearing. I was in earnest, like a preacher.

MRS KNOX. A preacher utters them in a reverent tone of voice.

MARGARET. I know: the tone that shews they don't

mean anything real to him. They usent to mean anything real to me. Now hell is as real to me as a turnip; and I suppose I shall always speak of it like that.

Anyhow, Ive been there; and it seems to me now that nothing is worth doing but redeeming people from it.

MRS KNOX. They are redeemed already if they choose to believe it.

MARGARET. Whats the use of that if they dont choose to believe it? You dont believe it yourself, or you wouldnt pay policemen to twist their arms. Whats the good of pretending? Thats all our respectability is, pretending, pretending, pretending. Thank heaven Ive had it knocked out of me once for all!

MRS KNOX. [greatly agitated] Margaret: dont talk like that. I cant bear to hear you talking wickedly. I can bear to hear the children of this world talking vainly and foolishly in the language of this world. But when I hear you justifying your wickedness in the words of grace, it's too horrible: it sounds like the devil making fun of religion. Ive tried to bring you up to learn the happiness of religion. Ive waited for you to find out that happiness is within ourselves and doesnt come from outward pleasures. Ive prayed oftener than you think that you might be enlightened. But if all my hopes and all my prayers are to come to this, that you mix up my very words and thoughts with the promptings of the devil, then I dont know what I shall do: I dont indeed: itll kill me.

MARGARET. You shouldnt have prayed for me to be enlightened if you didnt want me to be enlightened. If the truth were known, I suspect we all want our prayers to be answered only by halves: the agreeable halves. Your prayer didnt get answered by halves, mother. Youve got more than you bargained for in the way of enlightenment. I shall never be the same again. I shall never speak in the old way again. Ive been set free from this silly little hole of a house and all its pretences. I know now that I am stronger than you and Papa. I havnt found that happiness of yours that is within yourself; but Ive found strength. For good or evil I am set free; and none of the things that used to hold me can hold me now.

Knox comes back, unable to bear his suspense.

KNOX. How long more are you going to keep me waiting, Amelia? Do you think I'm made of iron? Whats the girl done? What are we going to do?

MRS KNOX. Shes beyond my control, Jo, and beyond yours. I cant even pray for her now; for I dont know rightly what to pray for.

KNOX. Dont talk nonsense, woman: is this a time for praying? Does anybody know? Thats what we have to consider now. If only we can keep it dark, I don't care for anything else.

MARGARET. Dont hope for that, father. Mind: I'll tell everybody. It ought to be told. It must be told.

KNOX. Hold your tongue, you young hussy; or go out of my house this instant.

MARGARET. I'm quite ready. [She takes her hat and turns to the door].

KNOX. [throwing himself in front of it] Here! where are you going?

MRS KNOX. [rising] You mustnt turn her out, Jo! I'll go with her if she goes.

KNOX. Who wants to turn her out? But is she going to ruin us? To let everybody know of her disgrace and shame? To tear me down from the position Ive made for myself and you by forty years hard struggling?

MARGARET. Yes: I'm going to tear it all down. It stands between us and everything. I'll tell everybody.

KNOX. Magsy, my child: dont bring down your father's hairs with sorrow to the grave. Theres only one thing I care about in the world: to keep this dark. I'm your father. I ask you here on my knees - in the dust, so to speak - not to let it out.

MARGARET. I'll tell everybody.

Knox collapses in despair. Mrs Knox tries to pray and cannot. Margaret stands inflexible.

ACT III

Again in the Gilbeys' dining-room. Afternoon. The table is not laid: it is draped in its ordinary cloth, with pen and ink, an exercise-book, and school-books on it. Bobby Gilbey is in the arm-chair, crouching over the fire, reading an illustrated paper. He is a pretty youth, of very suburban gentility, strong and manly enough by nature, but untrained and unsatisfactory, his parents having imagined that domestic restriction is what they call "bringing up." He has learnt nothing from it except a habit of evading it by deceit.

He gets up to ring the bell; then resumes his crouch. Juggins answers the bell.

BOBBY. Juggins.

JUGGINS. Sir?

BOBBY. [morosely sarcastic] Sir be blowed!

JUGGINS. [cheerfully] Not at all, sir.

BOBBY. I'm a gaol-bird: youre a respectable man.

JUGGINS. That doesnt matter, sir. Your father pays me to call you sir; and as I take the money, I keep my part of the bargain.

BOBBY. Would you call me sir if you wernt paid to do it?

JUGGINS. No, sir.

BOBBY. Ive been talking to Dora about you.

JUGGINS. Indeed, sir?

BOBBY. Yes. Dora says your name cant be Juggins, and that you have the manners of a gentleman. I always thought you hadnt any manners. Anyhow, your manners are different from the manners of a gentleman in my set.

JUGGINS. They would be, sir.

BOBBY. You dont feel disposed to be communicative on the subject of Dora's notion, I suppose.

JUGGINS. No, sir.

BOBBY. [throwing his paper on the floor and lifting his knees over the arm of the chair so as to turn towards the footman] It was part of your bargain that you were to valet me a bit, wasnt it?

JUGGINS. Yes, sir.

BOBBY. Well, can you tell me the proper way to get out of an engagement to a girl without getting into a row for breach of promise or behaving like a regular cad?

JUGGINS. No, sir. You cant get out of an engagement without behaving like a cad if the lady wishes to hold you to it.

BOBBY. But it wouldnt be for her happiness to marry me when I don't really care for her.

JUGGINS. Women dont always marry for happiness, sir. They often marry because they wish to be married women and not old maids.

BOBBY. Then what am I to do?

JUGGINS. Marry her, sir, or behave like a cad.

BOBBY. [Jumping up] Well, I wont marry her: thats flat. What would you do if you were in my place?

JUGGINS. I should tell the young lady that I found I couldnt fulfil my engagement.

BOBBY. But youd have to make some excuse, you know. I want to give it a gentlemanly turn: to say I'm not worthy of her, or something like that.

JUGGINS. That is not a gentlemanly turn, sir. Quite the contrary.

BOBBY. I dont see that at all. Do you mean that it's not exactly true?

JUGGINS. Not at all, sir.

BOBBY. I can say that no other girl can ever be to me what shes been. That would be quite true, because our circumstances have been rather exceptional; and she'll imagine I mean I'm fonder of her than I can ever be of anyone else. You see, Juggins, a gentleman has to think of a girl's feelings.

JUGGINS. If you wish to spare her feelings, sir, you can marry her. If you hurt her feelings by refusing, you had better not try to get credit for considerateness at the same time by pretending to spare them. She wont like it. And it will start an argument, of which you will get the worse.

BOBBY. But, you know, I'm not really worthy of her.

JUGGINS. Probably she never supposed you were, sir.

BOBBY. Oh, I say, Juggins, you are a pessimist.

JUGGINS. [preparing to go] Anything else, sir?

BOBBY. [querulously] You havnt been much use. [He wanders disconsolately across the room]. You generally put me up to the correct way of doing things.

JUGGINS. I assure you, sir, theres no correct way of jilting. It's not correct in itself.

BOBBY. [hopefully] I'll tell you what. I'll say I cant hold her to an engagement with a man whos been in quod. Thatll do it. [He seats himself on the table, relieved and confident].

JUGGINS. Very dangerous, sir. No woman will deny herself the romantic luxury of self-sacrifice and forgiveness when they take the form of doing something agreeable. Shes almost sure to say that your misfortune will draw her closer to you.

BOBBY. What a nuisance! I dont know what to do. You know, Juggins, your cool simple-minded way of doing it wouldnt go down in Denmark Hill.

JUGGINS. I daresay not, sir. No doubt youd prefer to make it look like an act of self-sacrifice for her sake on your part, or provoke her to break the engagement herself. Both plans have been tried repeatedly, but never with success, as far as my knowledge goes.

BOBBY. You have a devilish cool way of laying down the law. You know, in my class you have to wrap up things a bit. Denmark Hill isn't Camberwell, you know.

JUGGINS. I have noticed, sir, that Denmark Hill thinks that the higher you go in the social scale, the less sincerity is allowed; and that only tramps and riff-raff are quite sincere. Thats a mistake. Tramps are often shameless; but theyre never sincere. Swells - if I may use that convenient name for the upper classes - play much more with their cards on the table. If you tell the young lady that you want to jilt her, and she calls you a pig, the tone of the transaction may leave much to be desired; but itll be less Camberwellian than if you say youre not worthy.

BOBBY. Oh, I cant make you understand, Juggins. The girl isnt a scullery-maid. I want to do it delicately.

JUGGINS. A mistake, sir, believe me, if you are not a born artist in that line. - Beg pardon, sir, I think I heard the bell. [He goes out].

Bobby, much perplexed, shoves his hands into his pockets, and comes off the table, staring disconsolately straight before him; then goes reluctantly to his books, and sits down to write. Juggins returns.

JUGGINS. [announcing] Miss Knox.

Margaret comes in. Juggins withdraws.

MARGARET. Still grinding away for that Society of Arts examination, Bobby? Youll never pass.

BOBBY. [rising] No: I was just writing to you.

MARGARET. What about?

BOBBY. Oh, nothing. At least - How are you?

MARGARET. [passing round the other end of the table and putting down on it a copy of Lloyd's Weekly and her purse-bag] Quite well, thank you. How did you enjoy Brighton?

BOBBY. Brighton! I wasnt at - Oh yes, of course. Oh, pretty well. Is your aunt all right?

MARGARET. My aunt! I suppose so. I havent seen her for a month.

BOBBY. I thought you were down staying with her.

MARGARET. Oh! was that what they told you?

BOBBY. Yes. Why? Werent you really?

MARGARET. No. Ive something to tell you. Sit down and lets be comfortable.

She sits on the edge of the table. He sits beside her, and puts his arm wearily round her waist.

MARGARET. You neednt do that if you dont like, Bobby. Suppose we get off duty for the day, just to see what it's like.

BOBBY. Off duty? What do you mean?

MARGARET. You know very well what I mean. Bobby: did you ever care one little scrap for me in that sort of way? Dont funk answering: I dont care a bit for you - that way.

BOBBY. [removing his arm rather huffily] I beg your pardon, I'm sure. I thought you did.

MARGARET. Well, did you? Come! Dont be mean. Ive owned up. You can put it all on me if you like; but I dont believe you care any more than I do.

BOBBY. You mean weve been shoved into it rather by the pars and mars.

MARGARET. Yes.

BOBBY. Well, it's not that I dont care for you: in fact, no girl can ever be to me exactly what you are; but weve been brought up so much together that it feels more like brother and sister than - well, than the other thing, doesnt it?

MARGARET. Just so. How did you find out the difference?

BOBBY. [blushing] Oh, I say!

MARGARET. I found out from a Frenchman.

BOBBY. Oh, I say! [He comes off the table in his consternation].

MARGARET. Did you learn it from a Frenchwoman? You know you must have learnt it from somebody.

BOBBY. Not a Frenchwoman. Shes quite a nice woman. But shes been rather unfortunate. The daughter of a clergyman.

MARGARET. [startled] Oh, Bobby! That sort of woman!

BOBBY. What sort of woman?

MARGARET. You dont believe shes really a clergyman's daughter, do you, you silly boy? It's a stock joke.

BOBBY. Do you mean to say you dont believe me?

MARGARET. No: I mean to say I dont believe her.

BOBBY. [curious and interested, resuming his seat on the table beside her]. What do you know about her? What do you know about all this sort of thing?

MARGARET. What sort of thing, Bobby?

BOBBY. Well, about life.

MARGARET. Ive lived a lot since I saw you last. I wasnt at my aunt's. All that time that you were in Brighton, I mean.

BOBBY. I wasnt at Brighton, Meg. I'd better tell you: youre bound to find out sooner or later. [He begins his confession humbly, avoiding her gaze]. Meg: it's rather awful: youll think me no end of a beast. Ive been in prison.

MARGARET. You!

BOBBY. Yes, me. For being drunk and assaulting the police.

MARGARET. Do you mean to say that you - oh! this is a let-down for me. [She comes off the table and drops, disconsolate, into a chair at the end of it furthest from the hearth].

BOBBY. Of course I couldnt hold you to our engagement after that. I was writing to you to break it off. [He also descends from the table and makes slowly for the hearth]. You must think me an utter rotter.

MARGARET. Oh, has everybody been in prison for being drunk and assaulting the police? How long were you in?

BOBBY. A fortnight.

MARGARET. Thats what I was in for.

BOBBY. What are you talking about? In where?

MARGARET. In quod.

BOBBY. But I'm serious: I'm not rotting. Really and truly -

MARGARET. What did you do to the copper?

BOBBY. Nothing, absolutely nothing. He exaggerated grossly. I only laughed at him.

MARGARET. [jumping up, triumphant] Ive beaten you hollow. I knocked out two of his teeth. Ive got one of them. He sold it to me for ten shillings.

BOBBY. Now please do stop fooling, Meg. I tell you I'm not rotting. [He sits down in the armchair, rather sulkily].

MARGARET. [taking up the copy of Lloyd's Weekly and going to him] And I tell you I'm not either. Look! Heres a report of it. The daily papers are no good; but the Sunday papers are splendid. [She sits on the arm of the chair]. See! [Reading]: "Hardened at Eighteen. A quietly dressed, respectable-looking girl who refuses her name" - thats me.

BOBBY. [pausing a moment in his perusal] Do you mean to say that you went on the loose out of pure devilment?

MARGARET. I did no harm. I went to see a lovely dance. I picked up a nice man and went to have a dance myself. I cant imagine anything more innocent and more happy. All the bad part was done by other people: they did it out of pure devilment if you like. Anyhow, here we are, two gaolbirds, Bobby, disgraced forever. Isnt it a relief?

BOBBY. [rising stiffly] But you know, it's not the same for a girl. A man may do things a woman maynt. [He stands on the hearthrug with his back to the fire].

MARGARET. Are you scandalized, Bobby?

BOBBY. Well, you cant expect me to approve of it, can you, Meg? I never thought you were that sort of girl.

MARGARET. [rising indignantly] I'm not. You mustnt pretend to think that I'm a clergyman's daughter, Bobby.

BOBBY. I wish you wouldnt chaff about that. Dont forget the row you got into for letting out that you admired Juggins [she turns her back on him quickly] - a footman! And what about the Frenchman?

MARGARET. [facing him again] I know nothing about the Frenchman except that hes a very nice fellow and can swing his leg round like the hand of a clock and knock a policeman down with it. He was in Wormwood Scrubbs with you. I was in Holloway.

BOBBY. It's all very well to make light of it, Meg; but this is a bit thick, you know.

MARGARET. Do you feel you couldnt marry a woman whos been in prison?

BOBBY. [hastily] No. I never said that. It might even give a woman a greater claim on a man. Any girl, if she were thoughtless and a bit on, perhaps, might get into a scrape. Anyone who really understood her character could see there was no harm in it. But youre not the larky sort. At least you usent to be.

MARGARET. I'm not; and I never will be. [She walks straight up to him]. I didnt do it for a lark, Bob: I did it out of the very depths of my nature. I did it because I'm that sort of person. I did it in one of my religious fits. I'm hardened at eighteen, as they say. So what about the match, now?

BOBBY. Well, I dont think you can fairly hold me to it, Meg. Of course it would be ridiculous for me to set up to be shocked, or anything of that sort. I cant afford to throw stones at anybody; and I dont pretend to. I can understand a lark; I can forgive a slip; as long as it is understood that it is only a lark or a slip. But to go on the loose on principle; to talk about religion in connection with it; to - to - well, Meg, I do find that a bit thick, I must say. I hope youre not in earnest when you talk that way.

MARGARET. Bobby: youre no good. No good to me, anyhow.

BOBBY. [huffed] I'm sorry, Miss Knox.

MARGARET. Goodbye, Mr Gilbey. [She turns on her heel and goes to the other end of the table]. I suppose you wont introduce me to the clergyman's daughter.

BOBBY. I dont think she'd like it. There are limits, after all. [He sits down at the table, as if to to resume work at his books: a hint to her to go].

MARGARET. [on her way to the door] Ring the bell, Bobby; and tell Juggins to shew me out.

BOBBY. [reddening] I'm not a cad, Meg.

MARGARET. [coming to the table] Then do something nice to prevent us feeling mean about this afterwards. Youd better kiss me. You neednt ever do it again.

BOBBY. If I'm no good, I dont see what fun it would be for you.

MARGARET. Oh, it'd be no fun. If I wanted what you call fun, I should ask the Frenchman to kiss me - or Juggins.

BOBBY. [rising and retreating to the hearth] Oh, dont be disgusting, Meg. Dont be low.

MARGARET. [determinedly, preparing to use force] Now, I'll make you kiss me, just to punish you. [She seizes his wrist; pulls him off his balance; and gets her arm round his neck].

BOBBY. No. Stop. Leave go, will you.

Juggins appears at the door.

JUGGINS. Miss Delaney, Sir. [Dora comes in. Juggins goes out. Margaret hastily releases Bobby, and goes to the other side of the room.]

DORA. [through the door, to the departing Juggins] Well, you are a Juggins to shew me up when theres company. [To Margaret and Bobby] It's all right, dear: all right, old man: I'll wait in Juggins's pantry til youre disengaged.

MARGARET. Dont you know me?

DORA. [coming to the middle of the room and looking at her very attentively] Why, it's never No. 406!

MARGARET. Yes it is.

DORA. Well, I should never have known you out of the uniform. How did you get out? You were doing a month, wernt you?

MARGARET. My bloke paid the fine the day he got out himself.

DORA. A real gentleman! [Pointing to Bobby, who is staring open-mouthed] Look at him. He cant take it in.

BOBBY. I suppose you made her acquaintance in prison, Meg. But when it comes to talking about blokes and all that - well!

MARGARET. Oh, Ive learnt the language; and I like it. It's another barrier broken down.

BOBBY. It's not so much the language, Meg. But I think [he looks at Dora and stops].

MARGARET. [suddenly dangerous] What do you think, Bobby?

DORA. He thinks you oughtnt to be so free with me, dearie. It does him credit: he always was a gentleman, you know.

MARGARET. Does him credit! To insult you like that! Bobby: say that that wasnt what you meant.

BOBBY. I didnt say it was.

MARGARET. Well, deny that it was.

BOBBY. No. I wouldnt have said it in front of Dora; but I do think it's not quite the same thing my knowing her and you knowing her.

DORA. Of course it isnt, old man. [To Margaret] I'll just trot off and come back in half an hour. You two can make it up together. I'm really not fit company for you, dearie: I couldnt live up to you. [She turns to go].

MARGARET. Stop. Do you believe he could live up to me?

DORA. Well, I'll never say anything to stand between a girl and a respectable marriage, or to stop a decent lad from settling himself. I have a conscience; though I maynt be as particular as some.

MARGARET. You seem to me to be a very decent sort; and Bobby's behaving like a skunk.

BOBBY. [much ruffled] Nice language that!

DORA. Well, dearie, men have to do some awfully mean things to keep up their respectability. But you cant blame them for that, can you? Ive met Bobby walking with his mother; and of course he cut me dead. I wont pretend I liked it; but what could he do, poor dear?

MARGARET. And now he wants me to cut you dead to keep him in countenance. Well, I shant: not if my whole family were there. But I'll cut him dead if he doesnt treat you properly. [To Bobby, with a threatening move in his direction] I'll educate you, you young beast.

BOBBY. [furious, meeting her half way] Who are you calling a young beast?

MARGARET. You.

DORA. [peacemaking] Now, dearies!

BOBBY. If you dont take care, youll get your fat head jolly well clouted.

MARGARET. If you dont take care, the policeman's tooth will only be the beginning of a collection.

DORA. Now, loveys, be good.

Bobby, lost to all sense of adult dignity, puts out his tongue at Margaret. Margaret, equally furious, catches his protended countenance a box on the cheek. He hurls himself her. They wrestle.

BOBBY. Cat! I'll teach you.

MARGARET. Pig! Beast! [She forces him backwards on the table]. Now where are you?

DORA. [calling] Juggins, Juggins. Theyll murder one another.

JUGGINS. [throwing open the door, and announcing] Monsieur Duvallet.

Duvallet enters. Sudden cessation of hostilities, and dead silence. The combatants separate by the whole width of the room. Juggins withdraws.

DUVALLET. I fear I derange you.

MARGARET. Not at all. Bobby: you really are a beast: Monsieur Duvallet will think I'm always fighting.

DUVALLET. Practising jujitsu or the new Iceland wrestling. Admirable, Miss Knox. The athletic young Englishwoman is an example to all Europe. [Indicating Bobby] Your instructor, no doubt. Monsieur - [he bows].

BOBBY. [bowing awkwardly] How d'y' do?

MARGARET. [to Bobby] I'm so sorry, Bobby: I asked Monsieur Duvallet to call for me here; and I forgot to tell you. [Introducing] Monsieur Duvallet: Miss Four hundred and seven. Mr Bobby Gilbey. [Duvallet bows]. I really dont know how to explain our relationships. Bobby and I are like brother and sister.

DUVALLET. Perfectly. I noticed it.

MARGARET. Bobby and Miss - Miss-

DORA. Delaney, dear. [To Duvallet, bewitchingly] Darling Dora, to real friends.

MARGARET. Bobby and Dora are - are - well, not brother and sister.

DUVALLET. [with redoubled comprehension] Perfectly.

MARGARET. Bobby has spent the last fortnight in prison. You don't mind, do you?

DUVALLET. No, naturally. I have spent the last

fortnight in prison.

The conversation drops. Margaret renews it with an effort.

MARGARET. Dora has spent the last fortnight in prison.

DUVALLET. Quite so. I felicitate Mademoiselle on her enlargement.

DORA. Trop merci, as they say in Boulogne. No call to be stiff with one another, have we?

Juggins comes in.

JUGGINS. Beg pardon, sir. Mr and Mrs Gilbey are coming up the street.

DORA. Let me absquatulate [making for the door].

JUGGINS. If you wish to leave without being seen, you had better step into my pantry and leave afterwards.

DORA. Right oh! [She bursts into song]
    Hide me in the meat safe til the cop goes by.
    Hum the dear old music as his step draws nigh.
    [She goes out on tiptoe].

MARGARET. I wont stay here if she has to hide. I'll keep her company in the pantry. [She follows Dora].

BOBBY. Lets all go. We cant have any fun with the Mar here. I say, Juggins: you can give us tea in the pantry, cant you?

JUGGINS. Certainly, sir.

BOBBY. Right. Say nothing to my mother. You dont mind, Mr. Doovalley, do you?

DUVALLET. I shall be charmed.

BOBBY. Right you are. Come along. [At the door] Oh, by the way, Juggins, fetch down that concertina from my room, will you?

JUGGINS. Yes, sir. [Bobby goes out. Duvallet follows him to the door]. You understand, sir, that Miss Knox is a lady absolutely comme il faut?

DUVALLET. Perfectly. But the other?

JUGGINS. The other, sir, may be both charitably and accurately described in your native idiom as a daughter of joy.

DUVALLET. It is what I thought. These English domestic interiors are very interesting. [He goes out, followed by Juggins].

Presently Mr and Mrs Gilbey come in. They take their accustomed places: he on the hearthrug, she at the colder end of the table.

MRS GILBEY. Did you smell scent in the hall, Rob?

GILBEY. No, I didnt. And I dont want to smell it. Dont you go looking for trouble, Maria.

MRS GILBEY. [snuffing up the perfumed atmosphere] Shes been here. [Gilbey rings the bell]. What are you ringing for? Are you going to ask?

GILBEY. No, I'm not going to ask. Juggins said this morning he wanted to speak to me. If he likes to tell me, let him; but I'm not going to ask; and dont you either. [Juggins appears at the door]. You said you wanted to say something to me.

JUGGINS. When it would be convenient to you, sir.

GILBEY. Well, what is it?

MRS GILBEY. Oh, Juggins, we're expecting Mr and Mrs Knox to tea.

GILBEY. He knows that. [He sits down. Then, to Juggins] What is it?

JUGGINS. [advancing to the middle of the table] Would it inconvenience you, sir, if I was to give you a month's notice?

GILBEY. [taken aback] What! Why? Aint you satisfied?

JUGGINS. Perfectly, sir. It is not that I want to better myself, I assure you.

GILBEY. Well, what do you want to leave for, then? Do you want to worse yourself?

JUGGINS. No, sir. Ive been well treated in your most comfortable establishment; and I should be greatly distressed if you or Mrs Gilbey were to interpret my notice as an expression of dissatisfaction.

GILBEY. [paternally] Now you listen to me, Juggins. I'm an older man than you. Dont you throw out dirty water til you get in fresh. Dont get too big for your boots. Youre like all servants nowadays: you think youve only to hold up your finger to get the pick of half a dozen jobs. But you wont be treated everywhere as youre treated here. In bed every night before eleven; hardly a ring at the door except on Mrs Gilbey's day once a month; and no other manservant to interfere with you. It may be a bit quiet perhaps; but youre past the age of adventure. Take my advice: think over it. You suit me; and I'm prepared to make it suit you if youre dissatisfied - in reason, you know.

JUGGINS. I realize my advantages, sir; but Ive private reasons -

GILBEY. [cutting him short angrily and retiring to the hearthrug in dudgeon] Oh, I know. Very well: go. The sooner the better.

MRS GILBEY. Oh, not until we're suited. He must stay his month.

GILBEY. [sarcastic] Do you want to lose him his character, Maria? Do you think I dont see what it is? We're prison folk now. We've been in the police court. [To Juggins] Well, I suppose you know your own business best. I take your notice: you can go when your month is up, or sooner, if you like.

JUGGINS. Believe me, sir -

GILBEY. Thats enough: I dont want any excuses. I dont blame you. You can go downstairs now, if youve nothing else to trouble me about.

JUGGINS. I really cant leave it at that, sir. I assure you Ive no objection to young Mr Gilbey's going to prison. You may do six months yourself, sir, and welcome, without a word of remonstrance from me. I'm leaving solely because my brother, who has suffered a bereavement, and feels lonely, begs me to spend a few months with him until he gets over it.

GILBEY. And is he to keep you all that time? or are you to spend your savings in comforting him? Have some sense, man: how can you afford such things?

JUGGINS. My brother can afford to keep me, sir. The truth is, he objects to my being in service.

GILBEY. Is that any reason why you should be dependent on him? Don't do it, Juggins: pay your own way like an honest lad; and dont eat your brother's bread while youre able to earn your own.

JUGGINS. There is sound sense in that, sir. But unfortunately it is a tradition in my family that the younger brothers should spunge to a considerable extent on the eldest.

GILBEY. Then the sooner that tradition is broken, the better, my man.

JUGGINS. A Radical sentiment, sir. But an excellent one.

GILBEY. Radical! What do you mean? Dont you begin to take liberties, Juggins, now that you know we're loth to part with you. Your brother isnt a duke, you know.

JUGGINS. Unfortunately, he is, sir.

GILBEY. [together] What!

MRS GILBEY. [together] Juggins!

JUGGINS. Excuse me, sir: the bell. [He goes out].

GILBEY. [overwhelmed] Maria: did you understand him to say his brother was a duke?

MRS GILBEY. Fancy his condescending! Perhaps if youd offer to raise his wages and treat him as one of the family, he'd stay.

GILBEY. And have my own servant above me! Not me. Whats the world coming to? Heres Bobby and -

JUGGINS. [entering and announcing] Mr and Mrs Knox.

The Knoxes come in. Juggins takes two chairs from the wall and places them at the table, between the host and hostess. Then he withdraws.

MRS GILBEY. [to Mrs Knox] How are you, dear?

MRS KNOX. Nicely, thank you. Good evening, Mr Gilbey. [They shake hands; and she takes the chair nearest Mrs Gilbey. Mr Knox takes the other chair].

GILBEY. [sitting down] I was just saying, Knox, What is the world coming to?

KNOX. [appealing to his wife] What was I saying myself only this morning?

MRS KNOX. This is a strange time. I was never one to talk about the end of the world; but look at the things that have happened!

KNOX. Earthquakes!

GILBEY. San Francisco!

MRS GILBEY. Jamaica!

KNOX. Martinique!

GILBEY. Messina!

MRS GILBEY. The plague in China!

MRS KNOX. The floods in France!

GILBEY. My Bobby in Wormwood Scrubbs!

KNOX. Margaret in Holloway!

GILBEY. And now my footman tells me his brother's a duke!

KNOX. [together] No!

MRS KNOX. [together] Whats that?

GILBEY. Just before he let you in. A duke! Here has everything been respectable from the beginning of the world, as you may say, to the present day; and all of a sudden everything is turned upside down.

MRS KNOX. It's like in the book of Revelations. But I do say that unless people have happiness within themselves, all the earthquakes, all the floods, and all the prisons in the world cant make them really happy.

KNOX. It isnt alone the curious things that are happening, but the unnatural way people are taking them. Why, theres Margaret been in prison, and she hasnt time to go to all the invitations shes had from people that never asked her before.

GILBEY. I never knew we could live without being respectable.

MRS GILBEY. Oh, Rob, what a thing to say! Who says we're not respectable?

GILBEY. Well, it's not what I call respectable to have your children in and out of gaol.

KNOX. Oh come, Gilbey! we're not tramps because weve had, as it were, an accident.

GILBEY. It's no use, Knox: look it in the face. Did I ever tell you my father drank?

KNOX. No. But I knew it. Simmons told me.

GILBEY. Yes: he never could keep his mouth quiet: he told me your aunt was a kleptomaniac.

MRS KNOX. It wasnt true, Mr Gilbey. She used to pick up handkerchiefs if she saw them lying about; but you might trust her with untold silver.

GILBEY. My Uncle Phil was a teetotaller. My father used to say to me: Rob, he says, dont you ever have a weakness. If you find one getting a hold on you, make a merit of it, he says. Your Uncle Phil doesnt like spirits; and he makes a merit of it, and is chairman of the Blue Ribbon Committee. I do like spirits; and I make a merit of it, and I'm the King Cockatoo of the Convivial Cockatoos. Never put yourself in the wrong, he says. I used to boast about what a good boy Bobby was. Now I swank about what a dog he is; and it pleases people just as well. What a world it is!

KNOX. It turned my blood cold at first to hear Margaret telling people about Holloway; but it goes down better than her singing used to.

MRS KNOX. I never thought she sang right after all those lessons we paid for.

GILBEY. Lord, Knox, it was lucky you and me got let in together. I tell you straight, if it hadnt been for Bobby's disgrace, I'd have broke up the firm.

KNOX. I shouldnt have blamed you: I'd have done the same only for Margaret. Too much straightlacedness narrows a man's mind. Talking of that, what about those hygienic corset advertisements that Vines & Jackson want us to put in the window? I told Vines they werent decent and we couldnt shew them in our shop. I was pretty high with him. But what am I to say to him now if he comes and throws this business in our teeth?

GILBEY. Oh, put em in. We may as well go it a bit now.

MRS GILBEY. Youve been going it quite far enough, Rob. [To Mrs Knox] He wont get up in the mornings now: he that was always out of bed at seven to the tick!

MRS KNOX. You hear that, Jo? [To Mrs Gilbey] Hes taken to whisky and soda. A pint a week! And the beer the same as before!

KNOX. Oh, dont preach, old girl.

MRS KNOX. [To Mrs Gilbey] Thats a new name hes got for me. [to Knox] I tell you, Jo, this doesnt sit well on you. You may call it preaching if you like; but it's the truth for all that. I say that if youve happiness within yourself, you dont need to seek it outside, spending money on drink and theatres and bad company, and being miserable after all. You can sit at home and be happy; and you can work and be happy. If you have that in you, the spirit will set you free to do what you want and guide you to do right. But if you haven't got it, then youd best be respectable and stick to the ways that are marked out for you; for youve nothing else to keep you straight.

KNOX. [angrily] And is a man never to have a bit of fun? See whats come of it with your daughter! She was to be content with your happiness that youre always talking about; and how did the spirit guide her? To a month's hard for being drunk and assaulting the police. Did I ever assault the police?

MRS KNOX. You wouldnt have the courage. I dont blame the girl.

MRS GILBEY. [together] Oh, Maria! What are you saying?

GILBEY. [together] What! And you so pious!

MRS KNOX. She went where the spirit guided her.

And what harm there was in it she knew nothing about.

GILBEY. Oh, come, Mrs Knox! Girls are not so innocent as all that.

MRS KNOX. I dont say she was ignorant. But I do say that she didn't know what we know: I mean the way certain temptations get a sudden hold that no goodness nor self-control is any use against. She was saved from that, and had a rough lesson too; and I say it was no earthly protection that did that. But dont think, you two men, that youll be protected if you make what she did an excuse to go and do as youd like to do if it wasnt for fear of losing your characters. The spirit wont guide you, because it isnt in you; and it never had been: not in either of you.

GILBEY. [with ironic humility] I'm sure I'm obliged to you for your good opinion, Mrs Knox.

MRS KNOX. Well, I will say for you, Mr Gilbey, that youre better than my man here. Hes a bitter hard heathen, is my Jo, God help me! [She begins to cry quietly].

KNOX. Now, dont take on like that, Amelia. You know I always give in to you that you were right about religion. But one of us had to think of other things, or we'd have starved, we and the child.

MRS KNOX. How do you know youd have starved? All the other things might have been added unto you.

GILBEY. Come, Mrs Knox, dont tell me Knox is a sinner. I know better. I'm sure youd be the first to be sorry if anything was to happen to him.

KNOX. [bitterly to his wife] Youve always had some grudge against me; and nobody but yourself can understand what it is.

MRS KNOX. I wanted a man who had that happiness within himself. You made me think you had it; but it was nothing but being in love with me.

MRS GILBEY. And do you blame him for that?

MRS KNOX. I blame nobody. But let him not think he can walk by his own light. I tell him that if he gives up being respectable he'll go right down to the bottom of the hill. He has no powers inside himself to keep him steady; so let him cling to the powers outside him.

KNOX. [rising angrily] Who wants to give up being respectable? All this for a pint of whisky that lasted a week! How long would it have lasted Simmons, I wonder?

MRS KNOX. [gently] Oh, well, say no more, Jo. I wont plague you about it. [He sits down]. You never did understand; and you never will. Hardly anybody understands: even Margaret didnt til she went to prison. She does now; and I shall have a companion in the house after all these lonely years.

KNOX. [beginning to cry] I did all I could to make you happy. I never said a harsh word to you.

GILBEY. [rising indignantly] What right have you to treat a man like that? an honest respectable husband? as if he were dirt under your feet?

KNOX. Let her alone, Gilbey. [Gilbey sits down, but mutinously].

MRS KNOX. Well, you gave me all you could, Jo; and if it wasnt what I wanted, that wasnt your fault. But I'd rather have you as you were than since you took to whisky and soda.

KNOX. I dont want any whisky and soda. I'll take the pledge if you like.

MRS KNOX. No: you shall have your beer because you like it. The whisky was only brag. And if you and me are to remain friends, Mr Gilbey, youll get up to-morrow morning at seven.

GILBEY. [defiantly] Damme if I will! There!

MRS KNOX. [with gentle pity] How do you know, Mr Gilbey, what youll do to-morrow morning?

GILBEY. Why shouldnt I know? Are we children not to be let do what we like, and our own sons and daughters kicking their heels all over the place? [To Knox] I was never one to interfere between man and wife, Knox; but if Maria started ordering me about like that -

MRS GILBEY. Now dont be naughty, Rob. You know you mustnt set yourself up against religion?

GILBEY. Whos setting himself up against religion?

MRS KNOX. It doesnt matter whether you set yourself up against it or not, Mr. Gilbey. If it sets itself up against you, youll have to go the appointed way: it's no use quarrelling about it with me that am as great a sinner as yourself.

GILBEY. Oh, indeed! And who told you I was a sinner?

MRS GILBEY. Now, Rob, you know we are all sinners. What else is religion?

GILBEY. I say nothing against religion. I suppose were all sinners, in a manner of speaking; but I dont like to have it thrown at me as if I'd really done anything.

MRS GILBEY. Mrs Knox is speaking for your good, Rob.

GILBEY. Well, I dont like to be spoken to for my good. Would anybody like it?

MRS KNOX. Dont take offence where none is meant, Mr Gilbey. Talk about something else. No good ever comes of arguing about such things among the like of us.

KNOX. The like of us! Are you throwing it in our teeth that your people were in the wholesale and thought Knox and Gilbey wasnt good enough for you?

MRS KNOX. No, Jo: you know I'm not. What better were my people than yours, for all their pride? But Ive noticed it all my life: we're ignorant. We dont really know whats right and whats wrong. We're all right as long as things go on the way they always did. We bring our children up just as we were brought up; and we go to church or chapel just as our parents did; and we say what everybody says; and it goes on all right until something out of the way happens: theres a family quarrel, or one of the children goes wrong, or a father takes to drink, or an aunt goes mad, or one of us finds ourselves doing something we never thought we'd want to do. And then you know what happens: complaints and quarrels and huff and offence and bad language and bad temper and regular bewilderment as if Satan possessed us all. We find out then that with all our respectability and piety, weve no real religion and no way of telling right from wrong. Weve nothing but our habits; and when theyre upset, where are we? Just like Peter in the storm trying to walk on the water and finding he couldnt.

MRS GILBEY. [piously] Aye! He found out, didnt he?

GILBEY. [reverently] I never denied that youve a great intellect, Mrs Knox -

MRS KNOX. Oh get along with you, Gilbey, if you begin talking about my intellect. Give us some tea, Maria. Ive said my say; and Im sure I beg the company's pardon for being so long about it, and so disagreeable.

MRS GILBEY. Ring, Rob. [Gilbey rings]. Stop. Juggins will think we're ringing for him.

GILBEY. [appalled] It's too late. I rang before I thought of it.

MRS GILBEY. Step down and apologize, Rob.

KNOX. Is it him that you said was brother to a -

Juggins comes in with the tea-tray. All rise. He takes the tray to Mrs. Gilbey._

GILBEY. I didnt mean to ask you to do this, Mr Juggins. I wasn't thinking when I rang.

MRS GILBEY. [trying to take the tray from him] Let me, Juggins.

JUGGINS. Please sit down, madam. Allow me to discharge my duties just as usual, sir. I assure you that is the correct thing. [They sit down, ill at ease, whilst he places the tray on the table. He then goes out for the curate].

KNOX. [lowering his voice] Is this all right, Gilbey? Anybody may be the son of a duke, you know. Is he legitimate?

GILBEY. Good lord! I never thought of that.

Juggins returns with the cakes. They regard him with suspicion.

GILBEY. [whispering to Knox] You ask him.

KNOX. [to Juggins] Just a word with you, my man. Was your mother married to your father?

JUGGINS. I believe so, sir. I cant say from personal knowledge. It was before my time.

GILBEY. Well, but look here you know - [he hesitates].

JUGGINS. Yes, sir?

KNOX. I know whatll clinch it, Gilbey. You leave it to me. [To Juggins] Was your mother the duchess?

JUGGINS. Yes, sir. Quite correct, sir, I assure you. [To Mrs Gilbey] That is the milk, madam. [She has mistaken the jugs]. This is the water.

They stare at him in pitiable embarrassment.

MRS KNOX. What did I tell you? Heres something out of the common happening with a servant; and we none of us know how to behave.

JUGGINS. It's quite simple, madam. I'm a footman, and should be treated as a footman. [He proceeds calmly with his duties, handing round cups of tea as Mrs Knox fills them].

Shrieks of laughter from below stairs reach the ears of the company.

MRS GILBEY. Whats that noise? Is Master Bobby at home? I heard his laugh.

MRS KNOX. I'm sure I heard Margaret's.

GILBEY. Not a bit of it. It was that woman.

JUGGINS. I can explain, sir. I must ask you to excuse the liberty; but I'm entertaining a small party to tea in my pantry.

MRS GILBEY. But youre not entertaining Master Bobby?

JUGGINS. Yes, madam.

GILBEY. Who's with him?

JUGGINS. Miss Knox, sir.

GILBEY. Miss Knox! Are you sure? Is there anyone else?

JUGGINS. Only a French marine officer, sir, and - er - Miss Delaney. [He places Gilbey's tea on the table before him]. The lady that called about Master Bobby, sir.

KNOX. Do you mean to say theyre having a party all to themselves downstairs, and we having a party up here and knowing nothing about it?

JUGGINS. Yes, sir. I have to do a good deal of entertaining in the pantry for Master Bobby, sir.

GILBEY. Well, this is a nice state of things!

KNOX. Whats the meaning of it? What do they do it for?

JUGGINS. To enjoy themselves, sir, I should think.

MRS GILBEY. Enjoy themselves! Did ever anybody hear of such a thing?

GILBEY. Knox's daughter shewn into my pantry!

KNOX. Margaret mixing with a Frenchman and a footman - [Suddenly realizing that the footman is offering him cake.] She doesnt know about - about His Grace, you know.

MRS GILBEY. Perhaps she does. Does she, Mr Juggins?

JUGGINS. The other lady suspects me, madam. They call me Rudolph, or the Long Lost Heir.

MRS GILBEY. It's a much nicer name than Juggins. I think I'll call you by it, if you dont mind.

JUGGINS. Not at all, madam.

Roars of merriment from below.

GILBEY. Go and tell them to stop laughing. What right have they to make a noise like that?

JUGGINS. I asked them not to laugh so loudly, sir. But the French gentleman always sets them off again.

KNOX. Do you mean to tell me that my daughter laughs at a Frenchman's jokes?

GILBEY. We all know what French jokes are.

JUGGINS. Believe me: you do not, sir. The noise this afternoon has all been because the Frenchman said that the cat had whooping cough.

MRS GILBEY. [laughing heartily] Well, I never!

GILBEY. Dont be a fool, Maria. Look here, Knox: we cant let this go on. People cant be allowed to behave like this.

KNOX. Just what I say.

A concertina adds its music to the revelry.

MRS GILBEY. [excited] Thats the squiffer. Hes bought it for her.

GILBEY. Well, of all the scandalous - [Redoubled laughter from below].

KNOX. I'll put a stop to this. [He goes out to the landing and shouts] Margaret! [Sudden dead silence]. Margaret, I say!

MARGARET'S VOICE. Yes, father. Shall we all come up? We're dying to.

KNOX. Come up and be ashamed of yourselves, behaving like wild Indians.

DORA'S VOICE [screaming] Oh! oh! oh! Dont Bobby. Now - oh! [In headlong flight she dashes into and right across the room, breathless, and slightly abashed by the company]. I beg your pardon, Mrs Gilbey, for coming in like that; but whenever I go upstairs in front of Bobby, he pretends it's a cat biting my ankles; and I just must scream.

Bobby and Margaret enter rather more shyly, but evidently in high spirits. Bobby places himself near his father, on the hearthrug, and presently slips down into the arm-chair.

MARGARET. How do you do, Mrs. Gilbey? [She posts herself behind her mother].

Duvallet comes in behaving himself perfectly. Knox follows.

MARGARET. Oh - let me introduce. My friend Lieutenant Duvallet. Mrs Gilbey. Mr Gilbey. [Duvallet bows and sits down on Mr Knox's left, Juggins placing a chair for him].

DORA. Now, Bobby: introduce me: theres a dear.

BOBBY. [a little nervous about it; but trying to keep up his spirits] Miss Delaney: Mr and Mrs Knox. [Knox, as he resumes his seat, acknowledges the introduction suspiciously. Mrs Knox bows gravely, looking keenly at Dora and taking her measure without prejudice].

DORA. Pleased to meet you. [Juggins places the baby rocking-chair for her on Mrs Gilbey's right, opposite Mrs Knox]. Thank you. [She sits and turns to Mrs Gilbey] Bobby's given me the squiffer. [To the company generally] Do you know what theyve been doing downstairs? [She goes off into ecstasies of mirth]. Youd never guess. Theyve been trying to teach me table manners. The Lieutenant and Rudolph say I'm a regular pig. I'm sure I never knew there was anything wrong with me. But live and learn [to Gilbey] eh, old dear?

JUGGINS. Old dear is not correct, Miss Delaney. [He retires to the end of the sideboard nearest the door].

DORA. Oh get out! I must call a man something. He doesnt mind: do you, Charlie?

MRS GILBEY. His name isnt Charlie.

DORA. Excuse me. I call everybody Charlie.

JUGGINS. You mustnt.

DORA. Oh, if I were to mind you, I should have to hold my tongue altogether; and then how sorry youd be! Lord, how I do run on! Don't mind me, Mrs Gilbey.

KNOX. What I want to know is, whats to be the end of this? It's not for me to interfere between you and your son, Gilbey: he knows his own intentions best, no doubt, and perhaps has told them to you. But Ive my daughter to look after; and it's my duty as a parent to have a clear understanding about her. No good is ever done by beating about the bush. I ask Lieutenant - well, I dont speak French; and I cant pronounce the name -

MARGARET. Mr Duvallet, father.

KNOX. I ask Mr Doovalley what his intentions are.

MARGARET. Oh father: how can you?

DUVALLET. I'm afraid my knowledge of English is not enough to understand. Intentions? How?

MARGARET. He wants to know will you marry me.

MRS GILBEY.[together] What a thing to say!

KNOX. [together] Silence, miss.

DORA. [together] Well, thats straight, aint it?

DUVALLET. But I am married already. I have two daughters.

KNOX. [rising, virtuously indignant] You sit there after carrying on with my daughter, and tell me coolly youre married.

MARGARET. Papa: you really must not tell people that they sit there. [He sits down again sulkily].

DUVALLET. Pardon. Carrying on? What does that mean?

MARGARET. It means -

KNOX. [violently] Hold your tongue, you shameless young hussy. Dont you dare say what it means.

DUVALLET. [shrugging his shoulders] What does it mean, Rudolph?

MRS KNOX. If it's not proper for her to say, it's not proper for a man to say, either. Mr Doovalley: youre a married man with daughters. Would you let them go about with a stranger, as you are to us, without wanting to know whether he intended to behave honorably?

DUVALLET. Ah, madam, my daughters are French girls. That is very different. It would not be correct for a French girl to go about alone and speak to men as English and American girls do. That is why I so immensely admire the English people. You are so free – so unprejudiced - your women are so brave and frank - their minds are so - how do you say? - wholesome. I intend to have my daughters educated in England. Nowhere else in the world but in England could I have met at a Variety Theatre a charming young lady of perfect respectability, and enjoyed a dance with her at a public dancing saloon. And where else are women trained to box and knock out the teeth of policemen as a protest against injustice and violence? [Rising, with immense elan] Your daughter, madam, is superb. Your country is a model to the rest of Europe. If you were a Frenchman, stifled with prudery, hypocrisy and the tyranny of the family and the home, you would understand how an enlightened Frenchman admires and envies your freedom, your broadmindedness, and the fact that home life can hardly be said to exist in England. You have made an end of the despotism of the parent; the family council is unknown to you; everywhere in these islands one can enjoy the exhilarating, the soul-liberating spectacle of men quarrelling with their brothers, defying their fathers, refusing to speak to their mothers. In France we are not men: we are only sons - grown-up children. Here one is a human being - an end in himself. Oh, Mrs Knox, if only your military genius were equal to your moral genius - if that conquest of Europe by France which inaugurated the new age after the Revolution had only been an English conquest, how much more enlightened the world would have been now! We, alas, can only fight. France is unconquerable. We impose our narrow ideas, our prejudices, our obsolete institutions, our insufferable pedantry on the world by brute force - by that stupid quality of military heroism which shews how little we have evolved from the savage: nay, from the beast. We can charge like bulls; we can spring on our foes like gamecocks; when we are overpowered by reason, we can die fighting like rats. And we are foolish enough to be proud of it! Why should we be? Does the bull progress? Can you civilize the gamecock? Is there any future for the rat? We cant even fight intelligently: when we lose battles, it is because we have not sense enough to know when we are beaten. At Waterloo, had we known when we were beaten, we should have retreated; tried another plan; and won the battle. But no: we were too pigheaded to admit that there is anything impossible to a Frenchman: we were quite satisfied when our Marshals had six horses shot under them, and our stupid old grognards died fighting rather than surrender like reasonable beings. Think of your great Wellington: think of his inspiring words, when the lady asked him whether British soldiers ever ran away. "All soldiers run away, madam," he said; "but if there are supports for them to fall back on it does not matter." Think of your illustrious Nelson, always beaten on land, always victorious at sea, where his men could not run away. You are not dazzled and misled by false ideals of patriotic enthusiasm: your honest and sensible statesmen demand for England a two-power standard, even a three-power standard, frankly admitting that it is wise to fight three to one: whilst we, fools and braggarts as we are, declare that every Frenchman is a host in himself, and that when one Frenchman attacks three Englishmen he is guilty of an act of cowardice comparable to that of the man who strikes a woman. It is folly: it is nonsense: a Frenchman is not really stronger than a German, than an Italian, even than an Englishman. Sir: if all Frenchwomen were like your daughter - if all Frenchmen had the good sense, the power of seeing things as they really are, the calm judgment, the open mind, the philosophic grasp, the foresight and true courage, which are so natural to you as an Englishman that you are hardly conscious of possessing them, France would become the greatest nation in the world.

MARGARET. Three cheers for old England! [She shakes hands with him warmly].

BOBBY. Hurra-a-ay! And so say all of us.

Duvallet, having responded to Margaret's handshake with enthusiasm, kisses Juggins on both cheeks, and sinks into his chair, wiping his perspiring brow.

GILBEY. Well, this sort of talk is above me. Can you make anything out of it, Knox?

KNOX. The long and short of it seems to be that he cant lawfully marry my daughter, as he ought after going to prison with her.

DORA. I'm ready to marry Bobby, if that will be any satisfaction.

GILBEY. No you dont. Not if I know it.

MRS KNOX. He ought to, Mr Gilbey.

GILBEY. Well, if thats your religion, Amelia Knox, I want no more of it. Would you invite them to your house if he married her?

MRS KNOX. He ought to marry her whether or no.

BOBBY. I feel I ought to, Mrs Knox.

GILBEY. Hold your tongue. Mind your own business.

BOBBY. [wildly] If I'm not let marry her, I'll do something downright disgraceful. I'll enlist as a soldier.

JUGGINS. That is not a disgrace, sir.

BOBBY. Not for you, perhaps. But youre only a footman. I'm a gentleman.

MRS GILBEY. Dont dare to speak disrespectfully to Mr Rudolph, Bobby. For shame!

JUGGINS. [coming forward to the middle of the table] It is not gentlemanly to regard the service of your country as disgraceful. It is gentlemanly to marry the lady you make love to.

GILBEY. [aghast] My boy is to marry this woman and be a social outcast!

JUGGINS. Your boy and Miss Delaney will be inexorably condemned by respectable society to spend the rest of their days in precisely the sort of company they seem to like best and be most at home in.

KNOX. And my daughter? Whos to marry my daughter?

JUGGINS. Your daughter, sir, will probably marry whoever she makes up her mind to marry. She is a lady of very determined character.

KNOX. Yes: if he'd have her with her character gone. But who would? Youre the brother of a duke. Would -

BOBBY. [together] Whats that?

MARGARET. [together] Juggins a duke?

DUVALLET. [together] Comment!

DORA. [together] What did I tell you?

KNOX. Yes: the brother of a duke: thats what he is. [To Juggins] Well, would you marry her?

JUGGINS. I was about to propose that solution of your problem, Mr Knox.

MRS GILBEY. [together] Well I never!

KNOX. [together] D'ye mean it?

MRS KNOX. [together] Marry Margaret!

JUGGINS. [continuing] As an idle younger son, unable to support myself, or even to remain in the Guards in competition with the grandsons of American millionaires, I could not have aspired to Miss Knox's hand. But as a sober, honest, and industrious domestic servant, who has, I trust, given satisfaction to his employer [he bows to Mr Gilbey] I feel I am a man with a character. It is for Miss Knox to decide.

MARGARET. I got into a frightful row once for admiring you, Rudolph.

JUGGINS. I should have got into an equally frightful row myself, Miss, had I betrayed my admiration for you. I looked forward to those weekly dinners.

MRS KNOX. But why did a gentleman like you stoop to be a footman?

DORA. He stooped to conquer.

MARGARET. Shut up, Dora: I want to hear.

JUGGINS. I will explain; but only Mrs Knox will

understand. I once insulted a servant - rashly; for he was a sincere Christian. He rebuked me for trifling with a girl of his own class. I told him to remember what he was, and to whom he was speaking. He said God would remember. I discharged him on the spot.

GILBEY. Very properly.

KNOX. What right had he to mention such a thing to you?

MRS GILBEY. What are servants coming to?

MRS KNOX. Did it come true, what he said?

JUGGINS. It stuck like a poisoned arrow. It rankled for months. Then I gave in. I apprenticed myself to an old butler of ours who kept a hotel. He taught me my present business, and got me a place as footman with Mr Gilbey. If ever I meet that man again I shall be able to look him in the face.

MRS KNOX. Margaret: it's not on account of the duke: dukes are vanities. But take my advice and take him.

MARGARET. [slipping her arm through his] I have loved Juggins since the first day I beheld him. I felt instinctively he had been in the Guards. May he walk out with me, Mr Gilbey?

KNOX. Dont be vulgar, girl. Remember your new position. [To Juggins] I suppose youre serious about this, Mr - Mr Rudolph?

JUGGINS. I propose, with your permission, to begin

keeping company this afternoon, if Mrs Gilbey can spare me.

GILBEY. [in a gust of envy, to Bobby] Itll be long enough before youll marry the sister of a duke, you young good-for-nothing.

DORA. Dont fret, old dear. Rudolph will teach me high-class manners. I call it quite a happy ending: dont you, lieutenant?

DUVALLET. In France it would be impossible. But here - ah! [kissing his hand] la belle Angleterre!

EPILOGUE

Before the curtain. The Count, dazed and agitated, hurries to the 4 critics, as they rise, bored and weary, from their seats.

THE COUNT. Gentlemen: do not speak to me. I implore you to withhold your opinion. I am not strong enough to bear it. I could never have believed it. Is this a play? Is this in any sense of the word, Art? Is it agreeable? Can it conceivably do good to any human being? Is it delicate? Do such people really exist? Excuse me, gentlemen: I speak from a wounded heart. There are private reasons for my discomposure. This play implies obscure, unjust, unkind reproaches and menaces to all of us who are parents.

TROTTER. Pooh! you take it too seriously. After all, the thing has amusing passages. Dismiss the rest as impertinence.

THE COUNT. Mr Trotter: it is easy for you to play the pococurantist. [Trotter, amazed, repeats the first three syllables in his throat, making a noise like a pheasant]. You see hundreds of plays every year. But to me, who have never seen anything of this kind before, the effect of this play is terribly disquieting. Sir: if it had been what people call an immoral play, I shouldnt have minded a bit. [Vaughan is shocked]. Love beautifies every romance and justifies every audacity. [Bannal assents gravely]. But there are reticences which everybody should respect. There are decencies too subtle to be put into words, without which human society would be unbearable. People could not talk to one another as those people talk. No child could speak to its parent - no girl could speak to a youth - no human creature could tear down the veils - [Appealing to Vaughan, who is on his left flank, with Gunn between them] Could they, sir?

VAUGHAN. Well, I dont see that.

THE COUNT. You dont see it! dont feel it! [To Gunn] Sir: I appeal to you.

GUNN. [with studied weariness] It seems to me the most ordinary sort of old-fashioned Ibsenite drivel.

THE COUNT [turning to Trotter, who is on his right, between him and Bannal] Mr Trotter: will you tell me that you are not amazed, outraged, revolted, wounded in your deepest and holiest feelings by every word of this play, every tone, every implication; that you did not sit there shrinking in every fibre at the thought of what might come next?

TROTTER. Not a bit. Any clever modern girl could turn out that kind of thing by the yard.

THE COUNT. Then, sir, tomorrow I start for Venice, never to return. I must believe what you tell me. I perceive that you are not agitated, not surprised, not concerned; that my own horror (yes, gentlemen, horror - horror of the very soul) appears unaccountable to you, ludicrous, absurd, even to you, Mr Trotter, who are little younger than myself. Sir: if young people spoke to me like that, I should die of shame: I could not face it. I must go back. The world has passed me by and left me. Accept the apologies of an elderly and no doubt ridiculous admirer of the art of a bygone day, when there was still some beauty in the world and some delicate grace in family life. But I promised my daughter your opinion; and I must keep my word. Gentlemen: you are the choice and master spirits of this age: you walk through it without bewilderment and face its strange products without dismay. Pray deliver your verdict. Mr Bannal: you know that it is the custom at a Court Martial for the youngest officer present to deliver his judgment first; so that he may not be influenced by the authority of his elders. You are the youngest. What is your opinion of the play?

BANNAL. Well, whos it by?

THE COUNT. That is a secret for the present.

BANNAL. You dont expect me to know what to say about a play when I dont know who the author is, do you?

THE COUNT. Why not?

BANNAL. Why not! Why not!! Suppose you had to write about a play by Pinero and one by Jones! Would you say exactly the same thing about them?

THE COUNT. I presume not.

BANNAL. Then how could you write about them until you knew which was Pinero and which was Jones? Besides, what sort of play is this? That's what I want to know. Is it a comedy or a tragedy? Is it a farce or a melodrama? Is it repertory theatre tosh, or really straight paying stuff?

GUNN. Cant you tell from seeing it?

BANNAL. I can see it all right enough; but how am I to know how to take it? Is it serious, or is it spoof? If the author knows what his play is, let him tell us what it is. If he doesnt, he cant complain if I dont know either. I'm not the author.

THE COUNT. But is it a good play, Mr Bannal? Thats a simple question.

BANNAL. Simple enough when you know. If it's by a good author, it's a good play, naturally. That stands to reason. Who is the author? Tell me that; and I'll place the play for you to a hair's breadth.

THE COUNT. I'm sorry I'm not at liberty to divulge the author's name. The author desires that the play should be judged on its merits.

BANNAL. But what merits can it have except the author's merits? Who would you say it's by, Gunn?

GUNN. Well, who do you think? Here you have a rotten old-fashioned domestic melodrama acted by the usual stage puppets. The hero's a naval lieutenant. All melodramatic heroes are naval lieutenants. The heroine gets into trouble by defying the law (if she didnt get into trouble, thered be no drama) and plays for sympathy all the time as hard as she can. Her good old pious mother turns on her cruel father when hes going to put her out of the house, and says she'll go too. Then theres the comic relief: the comic shopkeeper, the comic shopkeeper's wife, the comic footman who turns out to be a duke in disguise, and the young scapegrace who gives the author his excuse for dragging in a fast young woman. All as old and stale as a fried fish shop on a winter morning.

THE COUNT. But -

GUNN [interrupting him] I know what youre going to say, Count. Youre going to say that the whole thing seems to you to be quite new and unusual and original. The naval lieutenant is a Frenchman who cracks up the English and runs down the French: the hackneyed old Shaw touch. The characters are second-rate middle class, instead of being dukes and millionaires. The heroine gets kicked through the mud: real mud. Theres no plot. All the old stage conventions and puppets without the old ingenuity and the old enjoyment. And a feeble air of intellectual pretentiousness kept up all through to persuade you that if the author hasnt written a good play it's because hes too clever to stoop to anything so commonplace. And you three experienced men have sat through all this, and cant tell me who wrote it! Why, the play bears the author's signature in every line.

BANNAL. Who?

GUNN. Granville Barker, of course. Why, old Gilbey is straight out of The Madras House.

BANNAL. Poor old Barker!

VAUGHAN. Utter nonsense! Cant you see the difference in style?

BANNAL. No.

VAUGHAN. [contemptuously] Do you know what style is?

BANNAL. Well, I suppose youd call Trotter's uniform style. But it's not my style - since you ask me.

VAUGHAN. To me it's perfectly plain who wrote that play. To begin with, it's intensely disagreeable. Therefore it's not by Barrie, in spite of the footman, who's cribbed from The Admirable Crichton. He was an earl, you may remember. You notice, too, the author's offensive habit of saying silly things that have no real sense in them when you come to examine them, just to set all the fools in the house giggling. Then what does it all come to? An attempt to expose the supposed hypocrisy of the Puritan middle class in England: people just as good as the author, anyhow. With, of course, the inevitable improper female: the Mrs Tanqueray, Iris, and so forth. Well, if you cant recognize the author of that, youve mistaken your professions: thats all I have to say.

BANNAL. Why are you so down on Pinero? And what about that touch that Gunn spotted? the Frenchman's long speech. I believe it's Shaw.

GUNN. Rubbish!

VAUGHAN. Rot! You may put that idea out of your head, Bannal. Poor as this play is, theres the note of passion in it. You feel somehow that beneath all the assumed levity of that poor waif and stray, she really loves Bobby and will be a good wife to him. Now Ive repeatedly proved that Shaw is physiologically incapable of the note of passion.

BANNAL. Yes, I know. Intellect without emotion. Thats right. I always say that myself. A giant brain, if you ask me; but no heart.

GUNN. Oh, shut up, Bannal. This crude medieval psychology of heart and brain - Shakespear would have called it liver and wits - is really schoolboyish. Surely weve had enough of second-hand Schopenhauer. Even such a played-out old back number as Ibsen would have been ashamed of it. Heart and brain, indeed!

VAUGHAN. You have neither one nor the other, Gunn. Youre decadent.

GUNN. Decadent! How I love that early Victorian word!

VAUGHAN. Well, at all events, you cant deny that the characters in this play were quite distinguishable from one another. That proves it's not by Shaw, because all Shaw's characters are himself: mere puppets stuck up to spout Shaw. It's only the actors that make them seem different.

BANNAL. There can be no doubt of that: everybody knows it. But Shaw doesnt write his plays as plays. All he wants to do is to insult everybody all round and set us talking about him.

TROTTER. [wearily] And naturally, here we are all talking about him. For heaven's sake, let us change the subject

VAUGHAN. Still, my articles about Shaw -

GUNN. Oh, stow it, Vaughan. Drop it. What Ive always told you about Shaw is -

BANNAL. There you go, Shaw, Shaw, Shaw! Do chuck it. If you want to know my opinion about Shaw -

TROTTER. [together] No, please, we dont.

VAUGHAN. [together] [yelling] Shut your head, Bannal.

GUNN. [together] Oh, do drop it.

The deafened Count puts his fingers in his ears and flies from the centre of the group to its outskirts, behind Vaughan.

BANNAL. [sulkily] Oh, very well. Sorry I spoke, I'm sure.

TROTTER. [beginning again simultaneously] Shaw -

VAUGHAN. [beginning again simultaneously] Shaw -

GUNN. [beginning again simultaneously] Shaw -

They are cut short by the entry of Fanny through the curtains. She is almost in tears.

FANNY. [coming between Trotter and Gunn] I'm so sorry, gentlemen. And it was such a success when I read it to the Cambridge Fabian Society!

TROTTER. Miss O'Dowda: I was about to tell these

gentlemen what I guessed before the curtain rose: that you are the author of the play. [General amazement and consternation].

FANNY. And you all think it beastly. You hate it. You think I'm a conceited idiot, and that I shall never be able to write anything decent.

She is almost weeping. A wave of sympathy carries away the critics.

VAUGHAN. No, no. Why, I was just saying that it must have been written by Pinero. Didnt I, Gunn?

FANNY. [enormously flattered] Really?

TROTTER. I thought Pinero was much too popular for the Cambridge Fabian Society.

FANNY. Oh yes, of course; but still - Oh, did you really say that, Mr Vaughan?

GUNN. I owe you an apology, Miss O'Dowda. I said it was by Barker.

FANNY. [radiant] Granville Barker! Oh, you couldnt really have thought it so fine as that.

BANNAL. I said Bernard Shaw.

FANNY. Oh, of course it would be a little like Bernard Shaw. The Fabian touch, you know.

BANNAL. [coming to her encouragingly] A jolly good little play, Miss O'Dowda. Mind: I dont say it's like one of Shakespear's - Hamlet or The Lady of Lyons, you know - but still, a firstrate little bit of work. [He shakes her hand].

GUNN. [following Bannal's example] I also, Miss O'Dowda. Capital. Charming. [He shakes hands].

VAUGHAN [with maudlin solemnity] Only be true to yourself, Miss O'Dowda. Keep serious. Give up making silly jokes. Sustain the note of passion. And youll do great things.

FANNY. You think I have a future?

TROTTER. You have a past, Miss O'Dowda.

FANNY. [looking apprehensively at her father] Sh-sh-sh!

THE COUNT. A past! What do you mean, Mr Trotter?

TROTTER. [to Fanny] You cant deceive me. That bit about the police was real. Youre a Suffraget, Miss O'Dowda. You were on that Deputation.

THE COUNT. Fanny: is this true?

FANNY. It is. I did a month with Lady Constance Lytton; and I'm prouder of it than I ever was of anything or ever shall be again.

TROTTER. Is that any reason why you should stuff naughty plays down my throat?

FANNY. Yes: itll teach you what it feels like to be forcibly fed.

THE COUNT. She will never return to Venice. I feel now as I felt when the Campanile fell.

Savoyard comes in through the curtains.

SAVOYARD. [to the Count] Would you mind coming to say a word of congratulation to the company? Theyre rather upset at having had no curtain call.

THE COUNT. Certainly, certainly. I'm afraid Ive been rather remiss. Let us go on the stage, gentlemen.

The curtains are drawn, revealing the last scene of the play and the actors on the stage. The Count, Savoyard, the critics, and Fanny join them, shaking hands and congratulating.

THE COUNT. Whatever we may think of the play, gentlemen, I'm sure you will agree with me that there can be only one opinion about the acting.

THE CRITICS. Hear, hear! [They start the applause].